DEAR MR SHAKESPEARE

July 12ᵗ 2013

To Joe –

With admiration and huge respect.

For Ken Ludwig
'the cause that wit is in other men'
(*Henry IV* Part 2)

SIMON READE

Dear Mr Shakespeare

LETTERS TO A JOBBING PLAYWRIGHT

Simon Reade.

OBERON BOOKS

LONDON

First published in 2009 by Oberon Books Ltd

521 Caledonian Road, London N7 9RH

Tel: 020 7607 3637 / Fax: 020 7607 3629

e-mail: info@oberonbooks.com

www.oberonbooks.com

Cover image of Shakespeare (the 'Chandos portrait') from HultonArchive (iStockphoto)

A catalogue record for this book is available from the British Library.

ISBN: 978-1-84002-829-4

Printed by CPI Antony Rowe, Chippenham, Wiltshire

CONTENTS

For the full effect of the emerging narrative of literary biography, this book should be read seamlessly. However, for quick reference, it can be dived into thus:

'If we present a mingle-mangle, our fault is to be excused, because the whole world is become a hodgepodge'

'Prologue', *Midas*, John Lyly, 1589

WILL	I love your early work. 'Was this the face that launched a thousand ships / And burnt the topless towers of Ilium?'
MARLOWE	I have a new one nearly done, and better. *The Massacre At Paris.*
WILL	Good title.
MARLOWE	And yours?
WILL	*Romeo and Ethel the Pirate's Daughter. (Beat, sighs despondently.)* Yes, I know.
MARLOWE	What is the story?
WILL	Well, there's a pirate... (*Confesses.*) In truth, I have not written a word.
MARLOWE	Romeo is... Italian. Always in and out of love.
WILL	Yes, that's good. Until he meets...
MARLOWE	Ethel.
WILL	Do you think?
MARLOWE	The daughter of his enemy.
WILL	(*Thoughtfully.*) The daughter of his enemy.
MARLOWE	His best friend is killed in a duel by Ethel's brother or something. His name is Mercutio.
WILL	Mercutio...good name.

Shakespeare in Love, Marc Norman and Tom Stoppard, 1998

JACK WARNER	This Shakespeare stuff ain't bad. I read some this morning and there are parts in English.
SAM WARNER	It's poison, Jackie.
HARRY WARNER	We'll lose a fortune.
SAM WARNER	Ya know the title ain't so bad. 'Shakespeare.' Sounds like a biopic.
JACK WARNER	It ain't called 'Shakespeare!'
ALBERT WARNER	Sam, it's called 'A Midsummer Night's Dream.'
SAM WARNER	Well that'll put us right in the crapper.
ALBERT WARNER	Maybe we should get a rewrite man.
HARRY WARNER	Mankiewitz is good.
ALBERT WARNER	Or Morrison.
SAM WARNER	Or pay this guy Shakespeare to do it.
ALBERT WARNER	He's dead, you idiot.
SAM WARNER	Then he'll cost us peanuts.

Shakespeare in Hollywood, Ken Ludwig, 2004

'How will this fadge?'
Viola, *Twelfth Night, or What You Will*, William Shakespeare, 1601

October 16th '88

Dear Mr Shagspur,

ARDEN OF FAVERSHAM

Thank you for sending us this play. However, as a theatre dealing with classical works and world theatre in translation, we do not accept unsolicited scripts of new plays by writers from England. I suggest that you send it to one of the many other theatres dedicated exclusively to new writing. Thank you for your interest in us.

Yours,

Melanie Topping

Literary Assistant

P.S. If you would like the script returned, then please send us the necessary postage. If we haven't heard from you within six weeks we will recycle the paper.

◇◇

November 1st '88

Dear Mr Sheikspar,

Thank you for your letter which Melly has passed on to me. To be honest, I don't really know your writing work, though I am familiar with your acting. So why don't you send me something to read?

Yours,

Percival Plover

Script Advisor

February 3ʳᵈ '89

Dear Mr Schaysopore,

I'm returning your scripts to you, sorry to have held onto them for so long. I don't want to have a general meeting because I find them of limited use. If you have a particular project you want to submit, then of course we will consider it. Having said that, when we hire writers to adapt underlying material, we tend towards people who have produced substantial original work themselves. Good luck with your Southwark show.

Yours,

Percival Plover
Associate Advisor (Scripts)

◇◇◇

September 3ʳᵈ '89

Dear Mr Shaaekspeer,

I've just seen *Arden of Faversham*. It's a shame I never had the opportunity to read it. On the playbill it doesn't credit an author, so inevitably people are wondering if it's by Thomas Kyd and/or Christopher Marlowe and/or a new-kid-on-the-block. But who gives a monkey's when the play itself is so good?

In the meantime, I'm looking forward to reading/hearing/ seeing more of that new kid's work/collaborations – even if composed under the guise of anonymity.

Yours,

Horatio J. Dowden-Adams
Assistant Literary Manager

October 1st '89

Dear Mr Shakespeen,

THE FAMOUS VICTORIES OF HENRY V

Thank you for sending us this chronicle play. Very enjoyable;
especially the zany character of Sir John Oldcastle. Did you
co-author this play with others in your acting company? It
does read like a collaborative, devised piece, if I'm honest:
well-researched by a committee, but not fully dramatised.
We need to get to know what makes the familiar characters
tic in the world of the play and who all the minor Lords and
Bishops really are. Then we will be able to distinguish one
from another, rather than just be reminded of the counties of
England.

Perhaps you could send me an original play?

Yours,

Horatio J. Dowden-Adams

Acting Literary Manager

◇◇

October 15th '89

Dear Mr Shaxpere,

AMLETH

You're right! What is an original play after all? The best
of dramatists, like all writers of fiction, have always been
magpies, stealing the bright bits from the nests of others
to feather their own. They rework stories, reinvent them,
and leave the dull bits and bobs they don't need. Those
three great Ancient Greek tragedians of the 5th century
BC – Aeschylus, Sophocles and the wilder Euripides – used
the mythological past as a perspective on their present by
plundering the Homeric myths of the 10th century BC. Most
dramatists have retold other people's stories ever since. It's

de rigeur amongst your contemporaries. Look at the way they delve into Ovid – who himself spun his extraordinary tales of transformation from ancient history, Greek myth and Roman folklore, from the stories of Babylon and Eastern civilization and from pagan legend.

If cribbing old texts for contemporary makeovers is original, then the reworking of *Amleth* is highly original. And intriguing. However, I'm not sure there's much of a hunger for ancient Icelandic myth shot through the Dark Age prism of Norse folklore. Would audiences buy it? Would theatre managements get it in the first place? And even if by some miracle they did, would they risk programming it? I doubt it. Perhaps we should be taking more of a lead in creating an appetite for new work? But we all know about the vagaries of the box office and the financial constraints of these conservative times. (Are there ever times in a theatre's economy which aren't conservative?)

We tend to feed the masses what they want (or those minority of the masses who come to the theatre at all) rather than what we believe they could/should feed upon. Or rather we feed them what we think they want, which is even more restricting and often underestimates the intelligence and adventure of our audiences. It's a circular argument. Our own lack of curiosity, and relying on ordering up variations on last season's hits, obeys a law of diminishing returns.

But I don't mean to depress you! I'm just being realistic about the prospects for *Amleth*, for all its black humour. (I particularly like the 'mad' hero revealing the eavesdropper in his Mum's boudoir, killing him, dismembering him, and feeding him to the pigs.)

The long and the short of it is that we wouldn't be able to commit to it here in the foreseeable future, not in the context of our current repertoire and the whims of the box office. But please do let me know of any future works.

Meanwhile, break a leg in Marlowe's new drama *The Jew of Malta* on Thursday.

Yours,

Horatio J. Dowden-Adams

Literary Manager Elect

◇◇

October 20th '89

Dear Mr Shagspere,

No, I didn't mean literally break a leg! I meant I hoped you'd get so much applause and have to take so many bows, so many curtain-calls, that the curtain went up and down so much that its legs – the internal structure which keeps the curtain stiff at the edges – broke. (I guess it doesn't make much sense if you don't have a curtain.)

Yours,

Horatio J. Dowden-Adams

Literary Manager

P.S. Do they have a curtain at The Curtain?

◇◇

November 11th '89

Dear Mr Shakespeare,

THE TAMING OF THE SHREW

I don't understand why you think we would commission your play if we know you are already writing it?

Yours,

Luke Strong

Artistic Director

January 7th '90

Dear Mr Shakespeare,

THE TAMING OF THE SHREW

What can I say? It's very funny. But it's a bit violent! I'm not against a bout of knockabout in the Italianate *commedia* tradition – but do you really want to get a reputation as a wife-beater so early in your career?

That said, I think we'd be happy to pursue it if you can confirm your intentions: do you intend it to be played stupid – using history, society, and context as our excuses? Or does it need a deeply ironic feminist perspective? And/or is Kate actually a true radical?

Yours,

Luke Strong

Artistic Director

cc Horatio J. Dowden-Adams

◇◇

February 2nd '90

Dear Mr Shakespeare,

THE TAMING OF THE SHREW

No, I don't think your intentions are entirely clear from the Induction scenes and their brief intervention shortly into the play proper.

Okay, so a Warwickshire tinker, knowingly called Christopher *Sly*, is debagged in his drunken slumber by a riot of toffs for a lark, and then dressed up in posh clothes, convincing Sly that he is a nob who has slept and dreamt for fifteen years, and is presented with "a pleasant comedy" (Induction ii).

But what does all this tell us about performing, or conforming to society's rules and regulations, or about inbred social status and so on, that you don't explore within the play itself?

And what about Kate's final speech? Here's a suggestion: why don't you add a stage direction at the end:

"She kneels before her husband, places her hand below her husband's foot, and then tips him over!"

That should stop any confusion! That would spare all our blushes. That should prevent any unlooked for controversy. After all, you wouldn't want this comedy to be remembered for all the wrong reasons, would you?

Best wishes,

Luke Strong

Artistic Director

P.S. Of course, you could just cut the speech…

◇◇

July 7th '91

Dear Mr Shakespeare,

HENRY VI

I've just seen your two-parter *Henry VI*. What a marathon!

The titles could be snappier:

> "The First Part of the Contention betwixt the two famous Houses of York and Lancaster, with the death of the good Duke Humphrey, and the Banishment and death of the Duke of Suffolk, and the Tragical end of the proud Cardinal of Winchester, with the notable Rebellion of Jack Cade: and the Duke of York's first claim unto the Crown…"

+

"The true Tragedy of Richard Duke of York and the death of good King Henry the Sixth, with the whole contention between the two Houses Lancaster and York..."

They don't do it for me, I'm afraid. But never judge a book by its cover!

I was aghast at the terrifyingly funny rottweiler Jack Cade aping the ruling classes, even down to his royal "We, John Cade", with his communist, tyrannical anarchy:

CADE ...There shall be no money; and all eat and drink on my score, and I will apparel them all in one livery, that they may agree like brothers, and worship me their lord.

DICK BUTCHER   The first thing we do, let's kill all the lawyers!
(*First Part of the Contention*, IVii)

"Kill all the lawyers!" Demented!

What you should do now is outdo Christopher Marlowe's *Tamburlaine* by giving us not two but three parts of the dynastic struggle – a story closer to home than Tamburlaine's conquest of the Middle East. Give us the sequel of King Richard III! It's crying out for it! You can't let your crook-backed Duke of Gloucester languish now. He is bursting to spew more from your imagination:

"Counting myself but bad till I be best ...
... I am myself alone." (*True Tragedy*, Vi)

Yours in admiration,

Sasha Radish

Producer

P.S. I don't mean to do Marlowe down, by the way. I'm sure you'd be the first to admit you're indebted to his epic vision and poetic rhetoric – as you are to those workmanlike chronicle plays in which you served your apprenticeship as an actor and rookie writer in the late '80s. But now you've really made the History Play your own.

◇◇

September 12th '91

Dear Mr Shakespeare,

Thanks for your suggestion about Henry VIII, but he is off target for us at the moment. We are on a strong Italian jaunt for the foreseeable future and we won't get back to a full pallet of programming for a while. Hope all is well with you.

Luke Strong

Artistic Director

◇◇

December 30th '91

Dear William Shakespeare,

THE TWO GENTLEMEN OF VERONA

You know I had misgivings about *The Taming of The Shrew*. Whenever I return to it, in the knowledge that there's *The Taming of A Shrew* doing the rounds, I do wonder whether you really wrote *The Shrew*! It doesn't sound like you; just a.n. other Elizabethan playmaker.

The Two Gentlemen of Verona, on the other hand, though undoubtedly influenced by the plays of John Lyly, has a distinctive voice I'm sure we'll hear more of in the future.

Taking your cue from your Italian *commedia dell'arte* sources, you place your comedies in Italian city states – which gives you a lot of freedom. They give you the licence to describe a whirlwind of romance on the one hand, and political intrigue on the other, without the initial distraction of your audience placing it within our own backyard (where, nonetheless, the whims of fate in love and romance, and political instability and social catastrophe, also play their role.) Italy is exotic – and, crucially, Catholic. By setting your plays there, you are being very risqué, quite subversive. In these fanatical, Protestant times, it's dynamite.

In *The Two Gentlemen of Verona*, there are a number of ideas you could develop in future:

- Parental pressure (Antonio's on his son, Proteus)
- The flibbertigibbet, unfaithful attraction of a male lover to another girl (Proteus from Julia to Silvia – I like his shape-changing, explicitly Ovidian name, by the way)
- A lover's stupidity (Valentine's)
- Banishment by the State (Valentine by the Duke)
- The stress of the city abandoned for a (harsh) rural idyll (I love those gentlemen outlaws, banished, like Valentine, for fits of passion committed for affairs of the heart)
- Disguise, especially of women as boys (Julia)
- The abandoned heroine (Julia).

You can also get more than Lyly does out of the lovers'

- Travels
- Midnight *rendezvous*
- Serenades
- Rope ladders (good prop)
- Confessors.

I also like the comic critique of their masters made by the servants Speed and Launce. But I'm worried about the dog. It will upstage everything else, you know. Although Launce's selfless love for his loveless dog Crab is parallel to Julia's for Proteus, and she might well adopt a similar hang-dog expression…

I think you'll look back on this play as a prototype, and that Valentine and Julia will breed many more lovesick heroes and cross-dressing, strong heroines in your plays to come.

Many thanks.

Yours,

Luke Strong

Artistic Director

cc Horatio J. Dowden-Adams

◇◇

March 3rd '92

Dear William,

TITUS ANDRONICUS

What is it? A play? A poem? A tragedy? A Romance? A Roman History play? It seems to be your imaginative response to your adventures in reading. And what reading! You are jamming with the classics, chiefly transforming Ovid's *Metamorphoses*.

You take his tale in which a wife, Procne, yearning for home and for her sister, Philomel, persuades her husband, Tereus, to sail across the seas to the lands of her father to fetch Philomel. Tereus returns empty-handed, claiming Philomel is dead. He's actually raped Philomel *en route* and abandoned her, preventing her from naming him as her attacker by hacking out her tongue. Yet Philomel weaves a tapestry depicting her abuse, which is brought to Procne:

"Weepe she could not. Ryght and wrong she reckeneth to
                                                confound,
And on revengement of the deede hir heart doth wholly
                                                ground."
                        (*Metamorphoses*, Book IV, transl. Golding)

Procne murders Itys, her and Tereus's son, and serves him up in a stew, which Tereus guzzles, before Procne confronts him with the indigestible truth. So driven to rage and despair and to the extremities of what it is to be human, she turns into a swallow, he into a Hoopoe, and Philomel into a nightingale.

19

In *Titus Andronicus* you go one better than Ovid by hacking off Lavinia's hands as well as her tongue, thus denying her Philomel's tools of communication:

> "A craftier Tereus, cousin, hast thou met
> And he hath cut those pretty fingers off
> That would have better sewed than Philomel." (IIiv)

It's thrilling stuff – moving, appalling, awesome.

Best wishes,

Luke Strong

Artistic Director

◇◇◇

April 4ᵗʰ '92

Dear Mr Shakespeare,

There are those who say that audiences need something extra-shocking because they're blasé about the violence of the cock- and dog-fight spectacle and the bear-baiting in the notorious low-life pits which share the environs of the stews, the back-alleys and the theatres; the ritualised violence of public executions; the hacked-off gargoyle-heads of traitors, spiked across London Bridge for all the world to gawp at and for crows to peck out their vile-jelly eyes. And in the theatre, Hieronimo bites out his own tongue most nights at The Rose in Kyd's **Spanish Tragedy**.

But in **Titus** you actually draw us away from the humdrum horror of everyday life and take us to a world of sensitive, limpid poetry – which you then violate. Maybe London is flocking to see it because they appreciate that the play's wanton acts of violence are symptomatic of a society corrupted, of a society on the brink of chaos? Rome, the once proud centre of brutal order, has disintegrated into a "wilderness of tigers" (IIIi), a place of madness. Or maybe they're pruriently pursuing your play's schlock horror notoriety?

Titus is your first tragedy. I suspect you're grappling with being a dramatic poet while learning how to be a poetic dramatist.

Yours,

Jonny Webster Junior
Actor/Dramatist

<><><><><><><><><><><><><><><><><><><><><><><><><><><><><><><><><><><><>

June 2nd '92

Dear Mr Shakespeare,

HENRY VI

Brilliant! A *pre*quel to make up a trilogy. You ve trumped Marlowe!

And it's a much better title: *The First Part of Henry VI*. Though you'll have to rename the other two now (*Part Two*, *Part Three*) and come up with a generic title like 'The Wars of the Roses', or something – not in deference to Henslowe's Rose Theatre where they have been premièred, but because of the scene plucking the Yorkist white rose against the Lancastrian red (IIiv):

"   Here I prophesy: this brawl today,
Grown to this faction in the Temple Garden,
Shall send between the Red Rose and the White
A thousand souls to death and deadly night."

(*HVI Pt1*, IIiv)

The pageant funeral of Henry V is a great image with which to begin the saga. Using that King's French conquests as the spur for your England v. France/Talbot v. Joan of Arc/heart v. head battle is very exciting.

I'm glad to hear that Thomas Nashe, together with George Peele and others, were able to help you out with additional writing at short notice. I guess you're burdened with commissions now and have to farm out some of the donkey-work. Presumably, you also had collaborators on what I'll now call *Henry VI Parts 2 and 3?* Researchers at least?

And a little bird tells me *Richard III is* in the pipeline too. You're on a roll.

Best wishes,

Sasha Radish

Producer

◇◇

June 18th '92

Dear William,

RICHARD III

Henry VI Parts 1, 2 + 3 and now a sequel: *Richard III*. Marlowe has yet to write a *trilogy*, let alone a *tetralogy* of four (if that's not a tautology?).

The script is a bit long, if I'm honest, so we'll need to talk about cuts. But you've really developed the possibilities of the soliloquy – all introspection by the end of the play after the extrovert button-holing of the audience at the start:

"Now is the winter of our discontent
Made glorious summer by this son of York…" (Ii)

It's electric, astonishing, a *tour de force*. Richard is unable to contain his glee at how he stage-manages events and controls people's lives. What I love is that you've developed Gloucester from *Henry VI* and exaggerated him still further for dazzling dramatic effect.

In *Titus* it appeared to some that you were emulating the Roman tragedies of Seneca, where grief is expressed rather than felt. But here you write impressionistic, psychologically revealing dialogue. When Richard woos Queen Anne over the corpse of

Henry VI, whom he has killed – along with her husband Edward, Prince of Wales – Richard offers Anne his sword so that she can take her revenge on him. She doesn't know what to do:

> "Nay, do not pause, 'twas I that killed your husband –
> But 'twas thy beauty that provoked me.
> Nay, now dispatch: 'twas I that stabbed young Edward –
> But 'twas thy heavenly face that set me on."

She drops the sword:

> "Take up the sword again, or take up me."

She takes up the latter. He pushes his luck:

RICHARD	Bid me kill myself and I will do it.
ANNE	I have already.
RICHARD	That was in thy rage... (Iii)

Richard is a consummate actor, versatile in his role-playing, audaciously getting away with black humour. Even he is incredulous:

> "Was ever woman in this humour wooed?
> Was ever woman in this humour won!" (Iii)

I enjoy Margaret being here still, in the court, a living ghost haunting the corridors of power, taunting them all, cursing away. She's all that unites them: in their collective guilt at having murdered her husband, Henry VI; and in their collective hatred of her (she was a hate figure throughout *Henry VI* after all). And in her language: picking up on the ritualistic repetitions of the other women in the play, she articulates the patterning of history:

> "I had an Edward, till a Richard killed him.
> I had a husband, till a Richard killed him.
> Thou hadst an Edward, till a Richard killed him.
> Thou hadst a Richard, till a Richard killed him." (IViv)

It's very particular, and yet at the same time you're saying that individuality disappears through the inevitable cycles of the historical process. You've bound up the personal and the political, the specific and the general. As all good drama can.

But cuts, William, cuts.

Best wishes,

Luke Strong

Artistic Director

<hr>

July 1st '92

Dear William,

EDWARD III

George Peele's done *Edward I*; Marlowe has given us *Edward II*; Heywood's working on *Edward IV*. (Eds you win, tales you lose, it seems.) And now I've got Peele, Marlowe, Thomas Kyd, Robert Greene, Michael Drayton and Robert Wilson on board for *Edward III*. It's going to be a smash. Would you like to join in too?

Best wishes,

Luke Strong

Artistic Director

P.S. If you don't like the idea of *Edward III*, you might like to think about a King Canute play, where another Ed, Edmund Ironside, rebels against the man who famously showed his court that even he wasn't capable of holding back the waves, nor thus the tide of history. You're good at rebellions: "Kill All The Lawyers!" (*HVI,Pt2*, IVii)

August 5th '92

Dear Mr Shakespeare,

A SONG

Thanks for sending me *A Song*:

> *"Shall I die? Shall I fly*
> *Lovers baits and deceits,*
> > *sorrow breeding?*
> *Shall I tend? Shall I send?*
> *Shall I sue, and not rue*
> > *my proceeding?"* etc.

Nice. (Although it tends to fold in on itself, don't you think?)

At present we don't need any more lyricists. Anyway, aren't plays more your thing than musicals?

Yours,

Sasha Radish

Producer

◇◇

MEMO

December 18th '92

From: Horatio Dowden-Adams, Literary Manager

To: Luke Strong, Artistic Director

Re: Edward III

Luke – in terms of our ongoing on-off love-affair/-hate-relationship with France, *Edward III* is spot on. In terms of the ruler over-stretching the state, it's exemplary. Edward battles on three fronts: at home with his courtiers; in the North against the King of Scotland; and across the Channel against John Valois, King of France. But his lust for power is sidetracked into the "idle dream" (IIii) of a powerful love-lust for the married Countess of Salisbury. Edward transforms into "a belly-god" with "lascivious wantonness" (IIIiii), a "love-sick cockney" (IIIiv). This cleverly enriches his character with moral dilemmas. It's a substantial, sexy sub-plot – crowd-pleasing. When Edward hires the court poet, Lodowick, to write wooing letters to the Countess on his behalf, it's very funny: Edward's royal ignorance of the conventions of poetry –

"I did not bid thee talk of chastity!" (IIi) –

in response to Lodowick's conventional opening gambit

"'More fair and chaste…'" (IIi)

There's also something psychologically revealing in Edward prevailing upon the Countess' father, Warwick, to be his pander. Warwick consents, but instantly feels remorse:

"Thus have I, in his majesty's behalf,
Apparelled sin in virtuous sentences." (IIi)

So Warwick comes out with the commonplace:

"Lilies that fester smell far worse than weeds" (IIi).

I also like the way Shakespeare shows that King Edward is a father too, impressing on his son, the Black Prince, the responsibility of leadership:

"   Ned, thou must begin
Now to forget thy study and thy books
And ure thy shoulders to an armour's weight." (Ii)

Then, at the centre of the play – as he's just done in *Richard III* – he gives us a citizens' scene commenting on the shenanigans of the rulers and their history-making quibbling:

"Edward is son unto our late king's sister
Where John Valois is three degrees removed" (IIIii),

says the well-informed First Citizen.

We should hold firm in our faith in Mr Shakespeare and support this play.

Horatio

December 28th '92

Dear William,

EDWARD III

I would rather you didn't take your name off the play. I fear the others will follow suit and that the prolific, ubiquitous author Anonymous will take all the credit.

What don't you like about it? There's so much here, so many seeds sown that could bear fruit in future history dramas, if you were so inclined, that I can't understand why you want to disown it? So, please reconsider your anonymity.

Yours truly,

Luke Strong

cc Horatio J. Dowden-Adams

P.S. Presumably you *don't* want your name attached to Robert Wilson's labour of love *Fair Em, The Miller's Daughter of Manchester*. I know you were there at the original script conference alongside Anthony Munday, but any association with it, however remote, won't do you any favours, believe me.

March 18ᵗʰ '93

Dear William,

A plague on this plague! Still, it will give you the chance to begin to develop the sonnet sequence you've been talking about.

I know the theatres are shut to stop the spread of infection…at least that's what they say. I thought the plague was spread by fleas parasiting on rats, not by theatregoers? The conspiracy theorist in me suspects that the powers that be feel threatened by these rabble-rousing plays – as they did in June last year when they temporarily suspended public performances.

Anyhow, can I recommend you use this dark period to further your reading of Ovid? Now *Venus & Adonis* has been published, you might like to look at *The Rape of Lucrece*. The contrast should appeal to your antithetical instincts.

Yours,

Manfred Mild

Poetry Editor

◇◇

April 20ᵗʰ '93

Dear William,

I know you are the only teenage boy to be married to an older woman in Warwickshire in living memory, but will your wife thank you for personifying her as the older love goddess, Venus, cradle-snatching the younger man, Adonis? Others might wonder further at you associating yourself with the epitome of male beauty.

Yours,

Richard B.

May 30th '93

Dear Mr Shakespeare,

The death of Marlowe, born in the same year as you,
must come as a terrible shock. You have both written
a similar number of plays and have each had your own
early successes. But he won't go on to flourish now as
you undoubtedly will. He's left us *The Jew of Malta*,
Tamburlaine Parts 1+2, *Edward II*, *Doctor Faustus*, *Dido
Queen of Carthage* (with Thomas Nashe) and *The Massacre
at Paris* (my particular favourite) as well as the poetry.

"From mine own ashes let a conqueror rise" (*Dido*, V)

Yours,

A Deptford Friend

◇◇

September 18th '93

William –

Your fellow Stratfordian *émigré* Richard Field, who published
Venus & Adonis, will also publish *The Rape of Lucrece*.

Yours,

Manfred Mild

Poetry Editor

◇◇

October 28th '93

Dear William,

THE RAPE OF LUCRECE

I'm not sure that it's wise to dedicate your second narrative
poem to your patron the Earl of Southampton in such terms:

"The love I dedicate to your lordship is without end…
What I have done is yours; what I have to do is yours;
being part in all I have, devoted yours."

Given that *Venus & Adonis* was also dedicated to him, please
reflect on the subject matter of each poem and then on the
conclusions to which people might leap. Not least your wife.

Yours,

Manfred Mild

Poetry Editor

◇◇

February 3rd '94

Dear Mr Shakespeare,

VENUS & ADONIS

Congratulations! I see *Venus & Adonis* has made it straight onto the
best-seller lists!

Best wishes!

Harriet Cumpton-Hawksley

Sales Manager

◇◇

4/3/94

Dear William,

As you know, we have recently re-branded ourselves as
the Royal National Classical Ensemble of New Works and
Devised Performance for the Lyric Playhouse and Found
Space (or R.N.C.E.N.W.D.P.L.P.F.S. for short). Our new
mission statement is: to treat new plays like classics, and
classics like new plays. So Luke, our Artistic Director, is

refreshing our Business Plan. It's been scoped, focus-grouped, and soon we hope to market-test various options for an Artistic Vision, if appropriate. As a result of a costly six month consultation imposed upon us by the public funding authorities, we have come up with a Strategy to complement our evolving, revolutionary Artistic Policy of radical classicism and classical radicalism. Luke no longer wants to champion <u>classical</u> new plays but classical <u>new</u> plays. (Call me old-fashioned and off-message, but personally I'm all in favour of classical new <u>plays</u>.)

I hope that's clear.

Best wishes,

Horatio J. Dowden-Adams

Literary Manager

R.N.C.E.N.W.D.P.L.P.F.S.

◇◇

July 6th '94

Dear William,

A MIDSUMMER NIGHT'S DREAM

Sorry it's taken so long to get back to you – that's the R.N.C.E.N.W.D.P.L.P.F.S. for you!

This letter is as hard for me to write as it will be for you to read, believe me. I'm afraid we just can't pursue your proposal for a new play in the context of our current repertoire. Luke and I think a dream play is a gorgeous idea and we've thought long and hard about it – probably longer than it would have taken you to deliver a first draft – but it's just not for us. I know this will be disappointing to you, and we have reached our difficult decision reluctantly, believe me; but I'm sure you will be able to place the play elsewhere and I, for one, will be green with envy when I attend the first night and read the notices.

With very best wishes,

Horatio J. Dowden-Adams

Literary Manager

◇◇

August 27th '94

Dear William,

THE COMEDY OF ERRORS – PROGRAMME NOTE

I have been asked to introduce your new play for the world première. As you know, it's notoriously difficult to prepare an audience in advance for a play that has yet to be proven on stage. So, rather than give them snippets of Roman source material, or pointers about twins in world drama, or the reputation of magic in the Mediterranean port of Ephesus – or even a treatise on time – I thought I could introduce *you*. I don't think it will do your profile any harm – and given that you've been out of action for a couple of years, certainly as far as the theatre-going public is concerned, while the playhouses have been shut throughout the Plague, I think it would be good to fanfare your return.

Here's what I had in mind:

WILLIAM SHAKESPEARE: A LIFE SO FAR

In Shakespeare's short but highly successful life so far as a poet, playwright and performer, he has managed to remain elusive. In some quarters he is already venerated, mythologised. For example, he neither confirms nor denies the precise date in April 1564 on which he was born, allowing us to conjecture it was auspiciously the 23rd, St George's Day, thus encouraging a cult of national sainthood: the Bard of England. Setting that aside, it's the human and political range of the plays that he has written, co-written or in which he has had a helping hand – plus his poems – that make this writer already worthy of such attention.

What we know of his life is fairly humdrum. He is the middle child of five (three other siblings didn't survive), the eldest son of: John Shakespeare, a glover and former local dignitary in Stratford-upon-Avon, Warwickshire; and Mary Arden, daughter of a wealthy farmer. He went to the local grammar school where he learned Latin and first read Plautus' plays *Amphitryo* and *Manaechmi* on which *The Comedy of Errors* is based. (In *Manaechmi*, Plautus just has one set of twins – Shakespeare ingeniously doubles that.)

Stratford is a prosperous market town in a pretty-ish part of the West Midlands, but not especially inspirational to a future dramatist. Shakespeare did, however, have his first experience of live theatre in its Guildhall where touring companies often perform, giving him a glimpse of the seedy glamour, majesty and magic of theatre, the itinerant lifestyle of its players and their liberal morals. He was stage-struck – and by the late 1580s he appears as an actor in London on the cusp of a writing career.

He's left a wife and three children behind him in Stratford. At the age of 18, he married an orphaned woman of independent means, Anne Hathaway, eight years his senior, already pregnant with his child. She gave birth to Susanna in 1583. Then the twins Judith and Hamnet were born in 1585. Shakespeare provides generously for them and returns to Stratford a few times a year – but London is now his playground. [*Is this par. too intrusive for Anne and the children?*]

London. A seductive city on the make. Shakespeare is opportunistic, full of self-belief. He lives a bachelor lifestyle in the high octane, media and literary circles of the metropolis – a boy from the sticks relishing being a man-about-town in the cornucopia of the big city. In theatre and poetry, he has discovered the art of the possible. When not performing, he spends his time dreaming up new realities.

He's a pretty good actor, taken on by the Lord Chamberlain's Men soon after he made his debut. But it's as a new writer that he's really making a splash. From the off, Shakespeare wrote fine blank verse, groundbreaking rhyme, and increasingly sophisticated prose. Between 1589 and 1592 he rattled off a pastiche classical tragedy packed with crowd-pleasing gore (*Titus Andronicus*) a couple of sex comedies influenced by John Lyly (the innovative *Two Gentlemen of Verona* and the controversial *Taming of the Shrew*) and a smash-hit, two-part chronicle of The Wars of the Roses. So successful were these history plays that he was commissioned to write not just a collaborative prequel (*Henry VI Part 1*) but a solo-authored sequel too: *Richard III*. No mean achievement for a young writer.

But, just as things were going so well, London was hit by the Plague. It has closed the theatres for two years. Undeterred, Shakespeare has turned to poetry, writing the Ovidian epics *Venus and Adonis* and *The Rape of Lucrece* during this period. And inspired by Sir Philip Sidney's posthumously published sonnet series *Atrophel and Stella* (1591), he's also been mapping out his own ambitious sonnet sequence.

Now, as the playhouses are re-opening and the audiences are flocking back, Shakespeare has written his pithiest, shortest, wittiest play to date: *The Comedy of Errors*, a play full of magic and transformation, loss and reconciliation, themes of Romance that this dramatist will surely pursue further in equivalent forms, with equal wonder, in the future.

The Comedy of Errors is a very serious piece of writing; yet it's been very funny watching it evolve. It plays to the groundlings, gawping like fish, one moment; and is psychologically introspective the next. Shakespeare writes impishly, deftly, but with sophistication and philosophical insight. It's a script which fires the imaginations of the performers, and will inspire the audience in the theatre. It has all the signs of a promising 30 year-old playwright getting into his stride.

What do you think?

Best wishes,

Horatio J. Dowden-Adams

Literary Manager

cc Loren Spiegelei, Literary Department Intern

◇◇◇

MEMO

October 8th '94

From: Luke Strong, Artistic Director

To: Bob Castle, Director

Re: COMEDY OF ERRORS, Shakespeare

Bob –

Shakespeare's *Comedy of Errors* is only funny when it's taken seriously. Don't jazz it up with snazzy biz. It is bewitching, enchanting; but its magic should be sinister. Don't forget Ephesus is associated with witchcraft for Elizabethans:

> "They say this town is full of cozenage,
> As nimble jugglers that deceive the eye,
> Dark-working sorcerers that change the mind,
> Soul-killing witches that deform the body…" (Iii)

And please don't be daft and go for the gimmick of having one actor play both Dromios, another both Antipholi. We have got to spot the differences for the confusion to work, even if the characters on stage don't, which is why they are confused:

> "Am I in earth, in heaven, or in hell?
> Sleeping or waking? Mad or well advised?
> Known unto these, and to myself disguised?" (IIii)

The final scene couldn't possibly work if you go down this doubling/halving route. You need the cute coda of the Dromios:

> "We came into the world like brother and brother,
> And now let's go hand in hand, not one before another." (V)

"Let's go hand in hand" – cue for a song?

Of course, you could have *more* than two of each set of twins: it would be great for a chase sequence if somehow three or four impossibly appeared in quick succession left, right and centre!

Luke

<><><><><><><><><><><><><><><><><><><><><><><><><><><><><><><><><><><><>

January 7ᵗʰ '95

Dear William,

LOVE'S LABOUR'S LOST

I don't want to knock your first piece of 'original' playwriting, rather than adaptation, to date. But I'm not sure what you're doing in this play. Or rather I'm not clear why you want to write such a parody? It's crammed with interminable flights of linguistic fantasy on the subject of love:

- the <u>aristocratic sonnet</u>, more in love with the sound of its own voice than it is with the girl;
- the <u>chivalric Spanish code</u> of so-called honourable love, which is Narcissistic;
- the pedantically <u>Latin-tagged lectures</u> from the sterile schoolmaster, Holfornes;
- the tell-it-as-it-is <u>rustic doggerel</u> of the clown, Costard.

Your purpose being, I guess, a precocious satire on the plays of Lyly and the later University Wits. People like Robert Greene. When he carped about you in his *Groatsworth of Wit*, it hurt you, didn't it?:

"There is an upstart Crow, beautified with our feathers, that with his *Tygers hart* wrapped in a *Players hyde*, supposes he is as well able to bombast out a blank verse as the best of you: and being an absolute *Johannes factotum*, is in his owne conceit the only Shake-scene in the countrey."

Okay, so it's below the belt to (ab)use a popular expression coined from your own play *Henry VI Part 3* (when the Duke of York attacks the sadism of Margaret):

"O tiger's heart wrapped in a woman's hide!" (liv)

But remember that Greene's scurrilous pamphlet was compiled and published posthumously – cowardly – by fellow dramatist Henry Chettle when the theatres were shut for the Plague at the end of autumn 1592. Their snobbish envy is clear in fingering you as "Johannes factotum" (a clever-dicky Latin moniker for Jack-of-All-Trades), as "an upstart Crow", "Shake-scene", a mere actor not a man with a Cambridge Master of Arts. Ignore them. Their ilk will always occupy a circle you never can – and why would you want to?

I fear your satire of their sort in *Love's Labour's* runs the risk of being an in-joke for the very cognoscenti you're satirising. Don't be hurt by Greene and the rest. You're bigger than them. And there are more of you now: like George Chapman who has arrived on the scene as a translator, even though he's not been to college; and Ben Jonson whose extensive classical knowledge seems to have been gleaned from the university of life, not Oxbridge. You are all a threat to the Greenes of this world. You all represent the rise of the middle classes, and you're having an impact on their world of arts and letters. Keep going!

Yours,

Luke Strong

Artistic Director

January 2nd '95

Dear William,

LOVE'S LABOUR'S LOST

The truth is, I find your play hard to like, even if (begrudgingly) I can admire it. In the end I too am a middle-class lad, like much of the public audience will be, and we despise toffs (whether this is out of jealousy is irrelevant). When the rich girl Princess of France turns her nose up at the King of Navarre's open-air court – "The wide fields too base to be mine" (II) – she's clearly forgotten her fur-lined booties.

As middle-classes, we will recognise something of ourselves in the ghastly, patronising, know-all Schoolmaster Holfornes and his sycophantic sidekick Sir Nathanial. But do we want to watch ourselves ridiculed like this on stage? We want to enjoy the comedy, not squirm. Where our hearts should die for the schoolmaster and his etiolating life, we just cringe.

I think that as a man now in his ageing 30s, you have tried to write a younger man's play. But there is something alienating in the arrogance of youth, don't you think?

What might attract people to the play? Berowne. He hypocritically chastises his friends' hypocrisy, who have all been doing what he's just been doing: writing love poetry, flouting their vows of chastity and dedicated study:

"   …Men of inconstancy.
When shall you see me write a thing in rhyme?
Or groan for Joan?" (IViii)

Hoisted by his own petard, he makes the assembled company admit that their love for *women* has made them abandon their studies:

"*They* are the books, the arts, the academes
That show, contain, and nourish all the world." (IViii)

You off-set high-brow wit, and Holfornes' middle-brow tiresomeness, with low-brow bawdry. Your clowns can be irritating at the best of times, if you don't mind me saying so. And the boisterous Costard with his knowing smirk isn't to my taste. But others will love him. Sometimes your plays speak to some people and not to others; and at other times to all of us in different ways. That's their universal appeal.

I think the play might work best in performance if:

1. it is mercilessly cut, mercifully for us, to two hours max. (including interval)
2. it's performed by comic geniuses – from Berowne to Costard to Holfornes – and then the two or three good (though long) scenes in it will shine and Berowne's story in particular will come across as very funny.

It will also be touching and moving when the Princess receives news of her father's death, interrupting the tone of the play and subverting the expectations of the genre – that there will be a resolution with marriages and reconciliations, and so on. It's daring. The play has loss in its title after all. It's all been futile. I quite like that:

> "Our wooing doth not end like an old play:
> Jack hath not Jill." (Vii)

With best wishes,

Luke Strong

Artistic Director

◇◇◇

May 4th '95

Dear Mr Shakespeare,

LOVE'S LABOUR'S WON

My name is Loren from the brave New World, and I'm the literary department's intern for this semester. Can I take this opportunity to say how much I admire your work. It's awesome!

Horatio J. is on vacation on annual leave and has asked me to rationalise his in-tray. I notice that he has scribbled some random notes to a new play of yours called *Love's Labour's Won*, and at the bottom of the page it says "see attached". But here's the thing: I don't seem to be able to find anything "attached", script or otherwise. I'm sorry to disturb you, sir, but I was wondering if it was important?

May I thank you for your attention and wish you a pleasant future.

Yours sincerely,

Loren Spiegelei

Intern to the Literary Manager

◇◇◇

June 20th '95

Dear William,

LOCRINE

So you're thinking of writing a play set in primitive Britain?

There's just been that silly chronicle play about *King Leir and his Three Daughters* that Henslowe commissioned at the Rose. A bit of a glib fleshing out of the passages in Spenser's *Faerie Queen*, and a trite happy ending. Anonymous, as ever.

How about looking at that old chestnut of the exiled Trojans being the founding fathers of England under King Locrine? Put in a bit of controversial male rape and you could call it *Trojans in Britain*.

Best wishes,

Sasha Radish

Producer

<><><><><><><><><><><><><><><><><><><><><><><><><><><><><><><><><><><><><>

July 12th '95

Dear William,

A MIDSUMMER NIGHT'S DREAM

This is wonderful. Why didn't you tell me about it before? A fantasy play in which authoritarian aristocrats, posh lovers, wrangling spirits and the lowly Peter Quince, Bottom and their "crew of patches" (IIIii) all publicly reveal their private dreams.

I also like the fact it sort of obeys the unities (okay, not of place, but of time), as if you needed to confine and constrain the parameters of your wild, anarchic, dream-like imagination. Theseus quite rightly celebrates the fact that

"The lunatic, the lover, and the poet
Are of imagination all compact." (V)

You should know, being all three!

Joking aside, it's an accessible play, celebrating the magic of humanity by showing it warts and all alongside humanised spirits. It's sexy. It's fun. It's poetic. It's clever. The kids will love it.

And I adore those fairies.

All best wishes,

Luke Strong

Artistic Director

41

July 14th '95

Dear William,

A MIDSUMMER NIGHT'S DREAM

I truly believe *A Midsummer Night's Dream* represents a turning-point in your career. Its structure alone is a technical *tour de force*: the two framing acts with Theseus and Hippolyta in Athens. And the entire plot in the wood, compacted into three acts that appear to flow effortlessly, but in fact are a miracle of construction. And then the poetry! Beautiful. Just beautiful.

Yours,

Horatio J. Dowden-Adams

Literary Manager

◇◇◇

August 20th '95

Dear Mr Shakespeare,

A MIDSUMMER NIGHT'S DREAM

I am writing to invite you to a symposium on Feminism in Renaissance Theatre Patriarchies that I am convening in association with the R.N.C.E.N.W.D.P.L.P.F.S.

In *A Midsummer Night's Dream* I admire the way the women challenge their oppressive patriarchy: Hermia her father's authoritarianism; a bruised but not broken Hippolyta nay-saying Theseus; Titania refusing to hand over to Oberon the Indian changeling boy she is rearing.

You're also very good on male (sexual) jealousy. Oberon is jealous of Titania's maternal instincts. Since he can not share them, he behaves like a spoilt, petulant boy and just wants to destroy, to take away her surrogate son for himself. He basically uses a kind of date-rape drug –

> "'   love-in-idleness…
> The juice of it on sleeping eyelids laid
> Will make or man or woman madly dote
> Upon the next live creature that it sees." (IIi)

So he gets Titania to sleep with an ass. And perversely gets off on it, pruriently spying on her fornicating with the hairy-faced, donkey-eared, penis-enlarged Bottom (IVi).

Egeus is so challenged by his daughter disobeying him by pursuing her young, virile lover, Lysander, against her father's will, that in his envy Egeus has to resort to the tyranny of the law:

> "I beg the ancient privilege of Athens:
> As she is mine, I may dispose of her –
> Which shall be either to this gentleman
> Or to her death, according to our law." (Ii)

Theseus supports these attempts to enforce Hermia's marriage to Demetrius:

> "To you your father should be as a god,
> One that composed your beauties, yea, and one
> To whom you are but as a form in wax,
> By him imprinted, and with his power
> To leave the figure or disfigure it." (Ii)

What about the mother's role in moulding the daughter? As in many of your other plays, it is significant that there are no mothers in *A Midsummer Night's Dream*. (As Titania says, being a "mortal" mother is fraught with the dangers of childbirth (IIi). Mothers who survive the ordeal are truly remarkable.)

Theseus is condoning violence against daughters – disfigurement the prerogative of fathers over their property-daughters. It's harsh and grotesque when we stop to think about it. Hermia asks Theseus what is

> "The worst that may befall me in this case
> If I refuse to wed Demetrius?" (Ii)

To which Theseus mercilessly replies:

> "Either to die the death, or to abjure
> For ever the society of men." (Ii)

What's he so scared of to threaten this young girl, on the cusp of sexually awakened womanhood, with the nunnery?:

> "To live a barren sister all your life,
> Chanting faint hymns to the cold, fruitless moon." (Ii)

He is afraid of her power to create. If men can control the wombs of women – the very thing that men can never have: the ability to grow life – then they will remain all-powerful. Their only alternative is to use their spiteful power to destroy life.

As much as male jealousy is debilitating, so too is unrequited, female obsession with men. Because women can not break free of men, and men won't let them go, a kind of sado-masochistic inter-dependence is played out by the four young lovers in the woods outside Athens:

> "I am sick when I do look on thee" (IIi),

Demetrius vilely attacks Helena; to which she replies, unrequited-love-sick:

> "And I am sick when I look not on you" (IIi):

> "I am your spaniel; and, Demetrius,
> The more you beat me, I will fawn on you:
> Use me but as your spaniel, spurn me, strike me,
> Neglect me, lose me; only give me leave,
> Unworthy as I am, to follow you.

What worser place can I beg in your love –
And yet a place of high respect with me –
Than to be used as you use your dog?" (IIi)

It's from a male perspective that the play celebrates marriage
with off-stage weddings and on-stage entertainment
before the off-stage consummations. Virginal women are
deflowered, hence so many emblematic botanical references.
Hippolyta, an Amazon, has been forced into marriage after
being defeated in battle by Theseus:

"Hippolyta, I wooed thee with my sword
And won thy love doing thee injuries.
But I will wed thee in another key,
With pomp, with triumph, and with revelling." (Ii)

Hippolyta's Amazonian qualities simultaneously attract and
repel an Alpha male like Theseus. In Hippolyta, you have
created the ultimate male fantasy. She is a tamed Amazon,
humiliated, nursing her wounds and harbouring her
resentments at having been denied her independence.

There's also much about young lads mistaking sexual arousal
for love. Lysander, for example, is fixated with "two bosoms":
he says it three times to Hermia; with another "bosom" to
Helena thrown in for good measure. He can't believe his luck
that here he is, in the middle of a chilly wood at night, alone
with Hermia:

"One turf shall serve as pillow for us both:
One heart, one bed, two bosoms, and one troth." (IIii)

Hermia's having none of it:

"Nay, good Lysander. For my sake, my dear,
Lie further off yet. Do not lie so near." (IIii)

Good girl! Egeus needn't have worried so much about his
daughter.

Anyhow, I hope you can see the tone of the paper I'm to deliver to the symposium. We would be greatly honoured by your presence.

Yours sincerely,

Rosita Sanchez

Professor of Renaissance Women's Studies

◇◇

August 21st '95

Dear Mr Shakespeare,

A MIDSUMMER NIGHT'S DREAM

I am writing to invite you to a symposium on Carnivalesque Subversion in the Plays of the '90s that I am convening in association with the R.N.C.E.N.W.D.P.L.P.F.S. I am particularly interested in exploring this with reference to the "rude mechanicals" (IIIii) of A Midsummer Night's Dream.

Although Quince, Bottom and their fellow artisan, am-dram performers do not wish to upset their royal patrons with their entertainment – indeed they are hopeful of a "sixpence a day" (IVii) royal pension for their efforts – they nonetheless undermine the supremacy of this world order and the very values it seeks to re-establish in celebrating the "nuptial hour" (Ii). In so doing, they expose the class prejudices of the ruling elite.

Peter Quince calls his play:

> "The Most Lamentable Comedy and Most Cruel Death of Pyramus and Thisbe." (Iii)

The courtiers scorn its subtitle:

> "'A tedious brief scene of young Pyramus
> And his love Thisbe: very tragical mirth'." (V)

And yet these are not the pretensions of ignorance on Quince's part. He is creating the very same new form of "comic lament" in his play-within-the-play of "simultaneous tragedy and laughter" that you are creating in your play, before our very eyes.

In *A Midsummer Night's Dream* our expectations of fulfilling comedic conventions – marriage, reconciliation, closure of the generation gap, happily-ever-after – are thwarted. Puck Robin has concluded Act III with the proverbial promise that

> "Jack shall have Jill,
> Nought shall go ill,
> The man shall have his mare again,
> And all shall be well." (IIIii)

Then twice we think the play has ended conventionally:

1) with the most powerful man on stage, Theseus, concluding with his couplet:

> "Away with us to Athens. Three and three,
> We'll hold a feast in great solemnity." (IVi)

2) with the conventional coda of the lovers wrapping things up :

> "Why then, we are awake. Let's follow him
> And by the way let us recount our dreams." (IVi)

But we have still to play out the mechanicals' plot:

> "Hard-hearted men that work in Athens here,
> Which never laboured in their minds till now." (V)

The court's condescension here has all the echoes of the aristocratic heckling of Holfornes' play at the end of *Love's Labour's Lost*: as with that play, we end up with a dim view of the ruling class. Theseus hurries them on to their "bergamask":

> "No epilogue, I pray you! For your play needs no excuse"
> (V).

But you have the last laugh on him by providing your play, with all its multiple false endings already (Theseus' solemn couplet; the lovers' coda; the bergamask; then Oberon and Titania's song of blessing) with puck Robin's epilogue, beginning with his excuse:

"If we shadows have offended..." (V)

I see where you're coming from. Do you see what I'm getting at?

Yours in comradeship,

Dr Chris Cole

Department of New Counter-Revisionist A-Historicism and Culturally Materialist Semiotic Liberalism

◇◇◇

August 30th '95

Dear Mr Shakespeare,

A MIDSUMMER NIGHT'S DREAM

A dream? Summery? "Hoary-headed frosts" (IIi)? "Angry winter" (IIi)?

I have been asked by my colleagues in the academy to contribute to their forthcoming symposia on your somewhat hallucinatory drama.

All the characters may wonder if they have been dreaming but their experiences have been drug-induced, spell-bound and/or the result of sleep-deprivation. The so-called 'dream' is more of a waking, emotional nightmare, Oberon's "accidents" (IVi) — whatever the aspirational dreams of lovers, of wannabe worker-actors.

Strictly speaking, there is only one dream: Hermia's:

"Help me, Lysander, help me! Do thy best
To pluck this crawling serpent from my breast! —
Ay me, for pity. What a dream was here?
Lysander, look how I do quake with fear.
Methought a serpent ate my heart away,
And you sat smiling at his cruel prey." (IIii)

It's a dream infected by the language of what has gone before:

"You spotted snakes with double tongue..." (IIii),

sang the fairies. And it infects Hermia's accusation that viper-like Demetrius has slain Lysander:

"Could not a worm, an adder do so much?
An adder did it, for with doubler tongue
Than thine, thou serpent, never adder strung." (IIIii)

Phallic, evil, deceitful.

As for the season, it is midsummer but upset by the warring jealousies of Titania/Oberon, of the discord between male/female, young/old which is played out in the turbulent, global warming of the weather:

"   ... The winds, piping to us in vain,
As in revenge have sucked up from the sea
Contagious fogs which, falling in the land,
Hath every pelting river made so proud
That they have overborne their continents." (IIi)

The play takes place under a full moon — lunar, lunacy, lunatic. A transformed Bottom observes to a "charmèd" Titania that

"Reason and love keep little company together nowadays."

(IIIi)

(When did they ever?)

"Lovers and madmen have such seething brains,
Such shaping fantasies, that apprehend
More than cool reason ever comprehends." (V)

49

Madness can also mean mad with bitter, raging anger.

Yours,

Nicholas Cobblestone

Institute of Thinking and Culture and New Ideologies

◇◇

September 30th '95

Dear Sir,

I hope this Lord Mayor of London petition to the Privy Council, against the theatres' "profane fables" causing "disorders and lewd demeanours which appear of late in young people of all degrees", will blow over. It's not caused by the plays in my view, but by the unseasonal rains that have wrecked the harvest, driving the rural workforce into the cities in pursuit of employment. Away from the firm hand and example of their country squires, they are unruled and unruly.

Yours faithfully,

A Correspondent from Clapham

◇◇

January 17th '96

Dear William,

ROMEO & JULIET

I like your opening Chorus. It's a teaser, whetting our appetite, telling us what the story is going to be and what's going to happen in the end:

> "A pair of star-crossed lovers take their life
> Whose misadventured piteous overthrows
> Doth with their death bury their parents' strife." (Prologue)

It's the 'why' and 'how' of the story and not the 'what' that matters. You keep reminding us of this. As Romeo heads off to gatecrash the Capulets' party he expresses "fear":

> "   My mind misgives
> Some consequence yet hanging in the stars
> Shall bitterly begin his fearful date
> With this night's revels, and expire the term
> Of a despisèd life closed in my breast
> By some vile forfeit of untimely death." (Iiv)

The machinations of fate; inauspicious stars; the mercantile greed of old men at the expense of priceless young love – the ingredients of a great, tragic love story.

Yours,

Luke Strong

Artistic Director

◇◇

January 25th '96

Dear Mr Shakespeare,

ROMEO & JULIET

Dr Chris Cole here again.

In your *Romeo & Juliet*, the love story is doomed from the outset by financial competition. The Capulets and the Montagues are of "Fair Verona" – a rich Italian city-state, familiar to us as a backdrop to your plays: it's where The Two Gentlemen are of; from whence Petruchio has come in *The Taming of the Shrew* (Iii). The Capulet and Montague families have as their models the Italian Renaissance banking dynasties: the Sforzas of Milan; the Medicis of Florence, being the most famous. So you invest their language with rich images of money:

"   Is she a Capulet?
O dear account! My life is my foe's debt" (Iv),

laments Romeo Montague (in disguise) when he learns of Juliet
Capulet's parentage after falling in love-at-first-sight with her at
Signor Capulet's revels.

The very first words spoken in this love story establish the
financial set-up:

"Two households, both alike in dignity" (Prologue)

However, more is made of the Capulet wealth and status
throughout, as if you've realised in the process of writing the
play that it will create more dramatic tension if Romeo and the
Montagues are seen as the (relatively) poorer family. "The great
rich Capulet," says Capulet's own comic servant (Iii). "The fair
daughter of rich Capulet," says Romeo (Iliii). Capulet himself
flaunts his wealth demanding "go hire me twenty cunning
cooks" for his daughter's imminent wedding feast; "spare not
for cost" he adds for good measure (IViv).

In such a context, Romeo absorbs the *lingua franca*. When we
first meet him he's being a simpering, egotistical, melancholic,
self-conceited unrequited lover, seemingly more in love with
the idea of love than the girl, Rosaline, moaning to his cousin
Benvolio with frustrated sexual desire:

"   She'll not be hit
With Cupid's arrow – she hath Dian's wit,
And in strong proof of chastity well armed;
From love's weak childish bow she lives unharmed.
She will not stay the siege of loving terms
Nor bide th'encounter of assailing eyes
Nor ope her lap to saint-seducing gold:
O, she is rich in beauty, only poor
That when she dies with beauty dies her store." (Ii)

Romeo debases the currency of love: she's so chaste that she
will not "ope her lap to saint-seducing gold" (Ii), won't spread

her legs, not even for "saint-seducing gold", for hard cash. This greatest love story ever told introduces the lover-boy protagonist as a cynic who's willing to pay to get his first fuck. (The Montagues' Samson and Gregory have already crudely quibbled about thrusting maids to the wall and cutting off their maidenheads. (Ii))

When Romeo first lays eyes on Juliet at her father's feast, his first impression is of a wealth of beauty. He asks a passing servant:

"What lady's that which doth enrich the hand
Of yonder knight?" (Iv)

(Conveniently, the hired-in caterer has no idea.) Romeo continues:

"O she doth teach the torches to burn bright!
Her beauty hangs upon the cheek of night
Like a rich jewel in an Ethiop's ear –
Beauty too rich for use, for earth too dear." (Iv)

To Juliet's face, Romeo can't hold back. He comes straight out with it:

"   Wert thou as fair
As that vast shore washed with the furthest sea,
I would adventure for such merchandise." (Iii)

"I'm a merchant venturer and my loved one's a commodity." Charming!

Juliet doesn't escape the language of commerce either, although she is dignified in her put-down to Romeo's relentless wordplay (the boy's excited: he's about to get married and therefore will get to "ope her lap" (Ii) as his right, *gratis*):

ROMEO   Let rich music's tongue
          Unfold th'imagined happiness that both
          Receive in either by this dear encounter.

JULIET   Conceit more rich in matter than in words

> Brags of his substance, not of ornament.
> They are but beggars that can count their worth,
> But my true love is grown to such excess
> I cannot sum up sum of half my wealth. (IIv)

When alone, Juliet can not stop the language of capital from penetrating her erotic imaginings:

> "O I have bought the mansion of a love
> But not possessed it; and though I am sold,
> Not yet enjoyed." (IIIii)

Poor little rich girl!

And it's not just the imagery of love and marriage that is tarnished. You even use the conventional punning of musicians about their "silver sound" to illustrate that in such a society art and poetry become a business transaction too. Your musician Simon Catling spells it out:

> "... I say 'silver sound', because musicians sound for silver!" (IVv)

They only play if they're paid.

Yet silver has less negative moral value in your image bank than gold. Gold can be "saint-seducing" (Ii). And gold is the agent of death. Romeo rails at the Friar for bringing him the news that he has been "banished" for killing Tybalt:

> "Thou cutt'st my head off with a golden axe." (IIIiii)

When he seeks out the "poor" (Vi) Apothecary to sell him illicit, under-the-counter poison, Romeo pays him accordingly:

> "There is thy gold, worse poison to men's souls,
> Doing more murders in this loathsome world
> Than these poor compounds thou mayst not sell.
> I sell thee poison: thou hast sold me none." (Vi)

In this context, how are we to take the ultimate battle of the Houses of Montague and Capulet? When they learn of the death of their children, when they see their suicide corpses in the Capulet mausoleum, they try to out-vie each other with conspicuous displays of their wealth, each promising to erect a "statue in pure gold" (Viii) of the other's offspring:

"There shall no figure at such rate be set
As that of true and faithful Juliet" (Viii),

says Montague. Then Capulet, wily banker that he is, seeks entry into the gold standard of the Exchange Rate Mechanism:

"As rich shall Romeo by his lady lie." (Viii)

Your play is a coruscating attack on the capitalist appropriation of the heart.

Yours in comradeship,

Dr Chris Cole

Department of Media Studies

cc Luke Strong

◇◇

MEMO

February 2nd '96

From: Luke Strong, Artistic Director

To: Dr Chris Cole

Re: ROMEO & JULIET, Shakespeare

Chris – what does all this teach us? That money can't buy love? That when we produce the play the performers should all be carrying financial journals and adding machines?

No. It tells us that any agenda, any blinkered reading of a play can prejudice our wider view of that play in performance. Plays, treated as literary texts, can be reduced to narrow, one-track-minded absurdity.

Plays are not for anaemic textual analysis alone, but for dramatic recreation. Shakespeare is a man of the *theatre*, not of the *lecture* theatre.

Luke Strong

◇◇

February 23rd '96

Dear William,

THE LAMENTABLE TRAGEDY OF ROMEO & JULIET

I've been thinking about your "lamentable tragedy" (your transformation of Arthur Brocke's dreary *Tragical History of Romeus & Juliet*).

In a world where we rely on visual images to communicate, where we receive a homogenised, globalised picture of the status quo, we are losing the ability to hear and to imagine for ourselves. If we can no longer see clearly then we won't think clearly either. In a world where we rant and rave our opinionated dogma and fundamentalism, we lack the humility of being able to listen. Your language is often thought a barrier to our understanding your plays, so your plays get big pictures plastered all over them. But perhaps we should be showing less of ourselves and hearing more of you. We can allow the sheer scale of your language to convey the small intensities of all our lives.

Wherever there are people there is conflict. We replicate our inner conflict in our society. And afterwards, we seek reconciliation and attempt to heal our wounds. That's what you're writing about in all your plays, it seems to me. That's the trajectory of your drama.

You've taken the tragedy of *Pyramus & Thisbe* from Ovid's *Metamorphoses* and rewritten the classic tale as contemporary drama. You use the story for painfully comic effect as an artisan-performed play at the Athenian Court in the play you've been writing in tandem, *A Midsummer Night's Dream*. Pyramus and Thisbe live on either side of a dividing wall, forbidden by their parents to communicate. But they flout the sanction of adult authority, and speak and kiss and love each other through a chink in that wall.

Those who erect walls are paranoid, are psychologically, politically and socially primitive. While they sustain their belief that the Enemy is on the Other side of the wall, while they project their fear into the unknown territory of the shadows, there will always be an endless cycle of fear and hatred. Ovid offers Pyramus & Thisbe; you offer Romeo & Juliet: two people who simply love each other, despite their impediments. That their stories will end tragically is known from the outset. But we need to keep challenging the artificial barriers that divide us. Through rejuvenating love, we will rediscover our common humanity.

Thank you for writing this play.

Yours,

Bob Castle

Director

◇◇

March 3rd '96

Dear William,

ROMEO & JULIET

We thought Romeo & Juliet was going to be a follow-up to A Midsummer Night's Dream. And there is great sex and great comedy – at least to start with. But don't you think it's a bit unfair on the audience to turn it towards tragedy so late in the day?

I've chatted with our sales guys and they definitely want you to stick to the original brief. It's a semi-populist, witty love story for the teen generation and their parents' sense of nostalgia. They want you to beef up the parts for the women because it's the women on the whole who motivate their husbands/lovers and kids to come to the theatre in the first place. We'll cast a couple of lookers for Tybalt and Mercutio; and Lady Capulet should have something for the

dads. We'll have to consider what to do about the snogging on stage in the schools' performances – there will be wolf-whistles!

This is what our guys think they can sell. The love interest is what makes it stand out from a lot of worthy dramas. Incidentally we have just been on a sales trip to America and there aren't many new plays being put on; but those that are, are generally screwball comedies featuring a dumb broad with legs. So don't make Juliet so brainy and please stay on course and think of the money!

June 1st delivery should be okay. After that we'll miss the potential Christmas market which is so important for adult/child cross-over titles like this. However, we need you to be firm on delivery dates because Charity, our Sales Manager, will want to start selling this title from Easter onwards. If you have something more to show her by then, it would help her to represent the play to the market.

William, it's very important that we get the play we commissioned. It's an oversubscribed market out there and what interests us and our investors about this title as commissioned is that it is different.

Oh, and how about a balcony so our "star-crossed lovers" (li) don't get to touch until after they're married?

All the best,

Lionel Farthing

Executive Producer

P.S. If you did it in modern dress, beefed up the lyrics, changed the dame's name to Maria, and put in a whole loada dance numbers, it'd make a great musical.

cc Charity Snicker, Sales and Marketing and Customer Interface

April 4ᵗʰ '96

Dear William,

"Two hours' traffic" (Prologue)? Who are you kidding! Play it that fast and we'll end up having a crash! I don't think anyone could perform Romeo & Juliet in two hours, not even with a gun to their head. So why have you lied? To convince managements it's a quickie, like The Comedy of Errors? Because you expect that we'll make loads of cuts? To gull the audience into staying through to the end?

Yours,

Lionel Farthing

Executive Producer

◇◇◇

September 15ᵗʰ '96

Dear William,

KING JOHN

I know you've already started working on *Richard II*, which, like *King John*, will be 99.9% in verse. But it's interesting that you're racing ahead with the historical throwback of *King John* first, as a kind of interim experiment. I can hear you trying out a shift in tone in this one-off play, before you tackle your next big swathe of contemporary history.

I like the way you hit the ground running:

KING JOHN	Now say, Chatillon, what would France with us?
CHATILLON	Thus, after greeting, speaks the King of France, In my behaviour, to the majesty, The borrowed majesty, of England here.
QUEEN ELEANOR	A strange beginning – "borrowed majesty"!
KING JOHN	Silence, good mother. Hear the embassy… (I)

You have the King of the title speak the first line of the play – not a soliloquy like in *Richard III*; John's not nearly so knowing, it's straight down to business. He's insulted by France. He tries to control his bossy Mum. And all within the first six lines. Bang on the nail!

I also like how you pile on the woes for England and for John. His claim to the throne is weak. With the death of his brother, King Richard The Lionheart, their young nephew, Arthur, has a stronger claim to the throne. And I like the fact you give Arthur an ambitious mum too:

QUEEN ELEANOR   Have I not ever said
                    How that ambitious Constance would not cease
                    Till she had kindled France and all the world
                    Upon the right and party of her son? (I)

And then on comes the Bastard, Philip Faulconbridge from Northants, to whom his own Mum reveals:

    "King Richard Coeur-de-lion was *thy* father." (I)

All these men with claims to the throne being stirred by their mothers! It's a great recipe for instability.

Best wishes,

Luke

◇◇

MEMO

September 18th '96

From: Horatio Dowden-Adams

To: Luke Strong

Re: KING JOHN

Luke – There's a morbidity in Shakespeare's new play. Death is a kind of character haunting the play – the impatient Bastard invokes him frequently:

>   "   Here's a stay
> That shakes the rotten carcass of old Death
> Out of his rags!" (II)

King John and his henchman, Hubert, circle the idea of
Death before taking five attempts to get through their one,
tentative, monosyllabic line of shared verse, agreeing to kill
Prince Arthur:

KING JOHN   He is a very serpent in my way,
             And whereso'er this foot of mine doth tread
             He lies before me. Dost thou understand me?
             Thou art his keeper.

HUBERT   And I'll keep him so
             That he shall not offend your majesty.

KING JOHN   Death.

HUBERT   My lord.

KING JOHN   A grave.

HUBERT   He shall not live.

KING JOHN   Enough.
                                                  (IIIiii)

(In *Richard III* there is a similar scene between Richard and
Buckingham, but Richard spits it out unequivocally:

> "Shall I speak plain? I wish the bastards dead."
>   (*RIII*, IVii))

In the middle of the play, Shakespeare changes gear.
Following on from the John/Hubert exchange, Arthur's
mother Constance comes on dishevelled and forlorn,
lamenting her "lost" son, Arthur:

> "Grief fills up the room of my absent child,
> Lies in his bed, walks up and down with me,
> Puts on his pretty looks, repeats his words,
> Remembers me of all his gracious parts,

Stuffs out his vacant garments with his form;
Then have I reason to be fond of grief?…
O Lord! My boy, my Arthur, my fair son!
My life, my joy, my food, my all the world!" (IIIiv)

She moves the Dauphin to despair:

"There's nothing in this world can make me joy.
Life is as tedious as a twice-told tale." (IIIiv)

I can't help feeling that Shakespeare's writing from personal
experience here. He has channelled his own grief over the
untimely death of his son, Hamnet, into Constance's lament
for her abducted child. Hamnet died while he was writing
this play. It's courageous and clearly spoken from the heart.

Horatio

◇◇

MEMO

September 19th '96

From: Horatio J. Dowden-Adams, Literary Manager

To: Lionel Farthing, Executive Producer

cc Luke Strong, Artistic Director

Re: THE LIFE AND DEATH OF KING JOHN

Lionel – Shakespeare calls his new play simply *The Life and
Death of King John*, which I guess does enough to differentiate
it from the two-parter of a couple of years ago *The Troublesome
Reign of King John*. I think we'll get away with cashing in on
the populist Protestant propaganda of that predecessor play.
When the Cardinal pops up out of the blue to spout the
Pope's fury, the way John spurns the Cardinal, Pope and
Catholic Church, is terrific:

"Tell him this tale, and from the mouth of England
Add this much more: that no Italian priest

> Shall tithe or toll in our dominions;
> But as we, under God, are supreme head,
> So, under Him, that great supremacy
> Where we do reign we will alone uphold,
> Without th'assistance of a mortal hand.
> So tell the Pope, all reverence set apart
> To him and his usurped authority." (IIIi)

An early English rebellion worthy of Henry VIII and the Reformation! And I like the irony of having John slag off another type of power-usurper when he's one himself. His headstrong zeal will not only set him on a collision course with the Pope, but on a road to self-destruction.

Horatio

◇◇◇

MEMO

September 21st '96

From: Horatio

To: Luke

Re: KJ

Luke – The endgame described by the Bastard plays out thus:

> "   England now is left
> To tug and scamble and to part by th'teeth
> The unowed interest of proud-swelling state.
> Now for the bare-picked bone of majesty
> Doth doggèd war bristle his angry crest
> And snarleth in the gentle eyes of peace;
> Now powers from home and discontents at home
> Meet in one line, and vast confusion waits
> As doth a raven on a sick-fallen beast,
> The imminent decay of wrested pomp." (IViii)

Shakespeare's allowed the Bastard to mature as the play progresses, from the lewd cheeky chappy with his incorrigible energy –

> "Zounds! I was never so bethumped with words
> Since I first called my brother's father Dad!" (II)

– to the sober King-maker, with a statesmanlike perspective on his country:

> "This England never did, nor never shall,
> Lie at the proud foot of a conqueror
> But when it did first help to wound itself.
> Now these her princes are come home again,
> Come the three corners of the world in arms
> And we shall shock them! Naught shall make us rue
> If England to itself do rest but true!" (Vvii)

Great words on which to end the play, "If" being the operative word.

The Bastard's journey is, in a way, the journey of the whole play. Shakespeare is bridging his writing from one kind of history play – the riproaring *Henry VI* kind echoed in *King John*'s early scenes – to another, more reflective kind, anticipated by the emotional power of *King John*'s final scenes: "This England". I expect he'll broaden his canvas in *Richard II* and beyond.

Horatio

◇◇

October 10ᵗʰ '96

Dear Mr Shakespeare,

I am happy to confirm that your family's Coat of Arms has, at long last, been granted. On his death, your father will pass it on to you; but may I remind you that since the death by drowning of your only son, Hamnet, in Stratford-upon-Avon in August, that you no longer have male issue to be the beneficiary after your death. Please would you inform my office should your circumstances alter in the meantime, so that we may amend the necessary paperwork.

Yours sincerely

Peregrine Cloten

pp Sir William Dethick

Garter King-of-Arms

◇◇

November 5th '96

Dear William,

Forgive me if I romanticise you writing at your desk in your garret, but you create such a seductive image of the struggling writer chucking his jottings in the fire in *King John* (as a metaphor for him watching his poisoned self die) that it sent a tingle down my spine:

> "I am a scribbled form, drawn with a pen
> Upon a parchment, and against this fire
> Do I shrink up." (Vvii)

Very moving.

Yours,

Horatio

◇◇

December 3rd '96

Dear Mr Holfornes,

Thank you for inviting the Creative Learning and Participation Department to comment on the playwright's process, for the edification of your students. We hear much about 'process' in our theatre-making now. The process in the rehearsal room. The actor's or director's process. William Shakespeare's process, for example, is a whirlwind of practicality which hardly allows space or time for what we think of as process. He writes swiftly, to commission. Once he's written his play, he'll read the entire thing out loud to the assembled company, doing all the voices. Then the management registers the play with the Master of the Revels to gain a formal licence. The theatre book-holder (a.k.a. prompter – like a Deputy Stage Manager 'on the book') will write out the parts: the characters' lines only, plus the cues. Hence Peter Quince's frustration with Flute's rehearsal process in *A Midsummer Night's Dream*:

"You speak your part at once, cues and all!" (IIIi)

(Actually, to be fair to Flute, he doesn't. Shakespeare's not bothered to write in those cues, assuming the actors would improvise, I guess.) Each of these parts is learnt by each actor separately. They will probably only gather together for one collective rehearsal/run-through before premièring a new play to the public. However, the leading actors will rehearse separately in private with their apprentices, hence the number of two-hander scenes written for the protagonist and his leading (boy) lady. Shakespeare is very practical.

What he would make of longer rehearsal periods, I don't know. Would he be flabbergasted, flattered, or just tell us to stop mucking around and get on with it?

Yours,

Jonty Trim

Life-Long Learning Leader + Outreach Origins Officer and Public Participation Practitioner

Detcembur 12th '96

Deer Mistar Shaikspeer,

I have seen three plays that you wroat. Loves Laibers Lost.
Midsummers Night Dreem. Roameeo and Jooleeyet.

Where did you get all your ideers from?

Howe old were you when you startid writing play's?

How old were you when you wroat Roameao and Joole-et?

Wich plays did you act in?

Where did you live when you wher six?

You are the most fabyooles person on earth.

From,

Lily Strong

Age 6

◇◇

December 15th '96

Dear Mr Shakespeare,

RICHARD II

Should you acknowledge the influence of the
anonymous *Thomas of Woodstock*, first performed
four years ago, by subtitling your new play
Richard II: or Thomas of Woodstock, Part 2?

Best,

Loren Spiegelei
Literary Intern

MEMO

December 16th '96

From: Horatio J. Dowden-Adams, Literary Manager

To: Luke Strong, Artistic Director

Re: RICHARD II

Luke – Don't be put off by the verse and the long
speeches and apparent formality of it all. I believe
Shakespeare's really delving here, as deep as he has since
Titus Andronicus.

He hasn't written a formal pageant. Why would he bother
with something so retrograde and dramatically inert? He has
written a passionate, political play. And a political Passion
play. It's there in the Christ-like Richard's big Abdication
Scene, a scene which alludes to "Judas", "Christ" and "Pilate"
(IV). And yet Richard also has absolute existential melt-
down:

"Are you contented to resign the crown?" (IV),

demands Bolingbroke. Richard prevaricates:

"I. No. No. Aye. For I must nothing be." (IV)

With "no name, no title" (IV), he is stripped of his very being.

Richard, like some Hindu renouncer or Christian ascetic,
offers to forgo his worldly goods and material possessions:

"I'll give my jewels for a set of beads,
My gorgeous palace for a hermitage,
My gay apparel for an almsman's gown,
My figured goblets for a dish of wood,
My sceptre for a palmer's walking staff,
My subjects for a pair of carvèd saints
And my large kingdom for a little grave,
A little, little grave, an obscure grave." (IIIiii)

His breakdown is all in public, which is what makes it feel
formal, I think. Surprisingly, Richard only has one soliloquy

in the entire play. It's almost the only soliloquy from any character (bar Salisbury's brief Choric lament (IIiv)). And although it's about soul-searching, he's still putting on a show, delivering his soliloquy directly to us, the audience: "Now, Sir" (Vv). He therefore intends, like everything else he and others say in the play, to have an effect on the listener. This direct relationship with the audience at this late point in the play will have quite an impact. Even in his most profound moment of introspection, on his dark night of the soul, Richard stays outside himself:

"I have been studying how I may compare
This prison where I live unto the world,
And for because the world is populous,
And here is not a creature but myself,
I can not do it. Yet I'll hammer it out." (Vv)

Richard pursues his "still breeding thoughts" (Vv) –

" These same thoughts people this little world
In humours like the people of this world" (Vv) –

like a dramatist of a medieval pageant peopling his play with the characters "Divine", "Ambition", "Content":

"Thus play I in one person many people,
And none contented... But whate'er I be,
Nor I, nor any man that but man is,
With nothing shall be pleased till he be eased
With being nothing." (Vv)

There is a magnificence in this nihilism, don't you think? But the existential pressure of just being is too much for Richard and he's driven almost mad. *Almost*, because discordant, jarring music brings him back from the edge. To him, the music is

" a sign of love, and love to Richard
Is a strange brooch in this all-hating world." (Vv)

He began his soliloquy with "I"; he ends it back with the self-deluding, royal, self-important and self-pitying third-person "Richard". How much has he learned?

Horatio.

◇◇

MEMO

December 18th '96

To: Luke

From: Horatio

Re: Richard II

"This teeming womb of royal kings" (IIi)

Think of *Richard II* in the context of Shakespeare's other History Plays. It's part of a grand design. Wombs. They represent women in his Histories, women defined by their function to breed heirs, preferably male ones. In *Edward III*, a womb is "the fragrant garden" (*EIII*, Iv). In *Richard III*, the opposite: Margaret describes Richard's mother's womb as a "kennel" from which the "hellhound" Richard has been unleashed (*RIII*, IViv). In *Richard II*, Queen Anne, in her metaphysical thinking, imagines:

> "Some unborn sorrow ripe in Fortune's womb
> Is coming towards me." (IIii)

She's a childless woman, and yet Shakespeare gives her a conception of childbirth:

> "   Thou art the midwife to my woe
> And Bolingbroke my sorrow's dismal heir.
> Now hath my soul brought forth her prodigy
> And I, a gasping new-delivered mother,
> Have woe to woe, sorrow to sorrow joined." (IIii)

The womb is a place of fecundity, but also a chilling nurturer of nothing in this play.

" Your fair discourse hath been as sugar, Making the hard way sweet and delectable" (IIiii)

I know the language in *Richard II* might put some people off, but... When Mowbray, Duke of Norfolk is banished from England for his involvement in Thomas of Woodstock's assassination, "never to return" (Iiii), he likens banishment to losing the power of speech:

"The language I have learnt these forty years,
My native English, now must I forgo
And now my tongue's use is to me no more
Than an unstringèd viol or a harp...
Within my mouth you have engaoled my tongue,
Doubly portcullised with my teeth and lips
And dull unfeeling barren ignorance
Is made my gaoler to attend on me...
What is thy sentence then but speechless death
Which robs my tongue from breathing native breath?"
(Iiii)

Sure, there's an Elizabethan, courtly formality in the language here which harnesses the emotion; but at the same time it shows how we are trapped in language, just at the point we need to be emotional. John of Gaunt says as much when he upbraids his son, Bolingbroke, for not speaking from the heart when he is also banished by Richard:

"O, to what purpose dost thou hoard thy words?" (Iiii)

Gaunt develops his theme later:

"Oh, but they say the tongues of dying men
Enforce attention like deep harmony.
Where words are scarce they are seldom spent in vain
For they breathe truth that breathe their words in pain."
(IIi)

And he goes on to deliver the great rhetoric of:

"Methinks I am a prophet new inspired" (IIi),

with a twenty-one line sentence beginning

"This royal throne of kings, this sceptred isle…" (IIi),

only reaching its verb in the 20th line "*Is* now leased out" (IIi)!

> "   **Our eyes do hate the dire aspect**
> **Of civil wounds plough'd up with neighbour's**
> **sword" (Iiii)**

The play's got real political edge too. The ultimate prophesy in the play comes from the awkward Bishop of Carlisle, who is dead against the coronation of Bolingbroke:

> "And if you crown him let me prophesy:
> The blood of English shall manure the ground
> And future ages groan for this foul act.
> Peace shall go sleep with Turks and infidels;
> And in this seat of peace, tumultuous wars
> Shall kin with kin and kind with kind confound.
> Disorder, horror, fear and mutiny
> Shall here inherit, and this land be called
> The field of Golgotha and dead men's skulls.
> Oh, if you raise this house against this house
> It will the woefullest division prove
> That ever fell upon this cursèd earth." (IV)

Shakespeare chronicled this Armageddon in the *Henry VI* and *Richard III* plays. He touched upon it in *King John*. As he embarks upon his next round of History Plays, he's put the summation of the whole grand design into Carlisle's prophetic mouth. I bet he's got Carlisle's speech pinned above his writing desk!

The killing of kings is a kind of pagan Ur-Myth, a necessary act to enable us to emerge from the bleak discontented winter of the past and sow the new spring seeds of the future for a glorious summer. What Shakespeare presents is a tale in which the killing of the king is a necessity: a political necessity; an existential necessity; and, in their self-dramatising world, a tragic necessity for the characters. It's dynamite.

He hasn't really written a Christian allegory after all, despite the Passion play trappings. There is no resurrection, no redemption, little hope. The over-riding mood is one of gloom and doom, but deeply satisfying – cathartic, like a Greek tragedy.

Shakespeare has now ventured so far on this journey, his own pilgrimage, that now he's beavering away at *Henry IV*, to redeem mankind in all its glorious, gorgeous humanity.

Roll on Hal and Falstaff!

Horatio J. Dowden-Adams

◇◇

MEMORANDUM

December 27th '96

From: Luke

To: Horatio

Horatio – is *The Merchant of Venice* a racist, anti-Semitic play? Or is it about vile anti-Semites, homophobes, intolerance and greed? Or, as ever with Shakespeare, is it equivocal?

Luke

MEMO

December 28th '96

From: Horatio J. Dowden-Adams, Dramaturg

To: Luke Strong, Artistic Director

Re: THE MERCHANT OF VENICE

Luke –

I have no doubt that the play can be produced as *anti*-anti-Semitic, and more generally as a play about prejudice in all its guises, rather than as a prejudiced play in itself. Whatever our own religion and our own persecutions, "Hath not a Jew eyes?" etc. (IIIi) makes all humanity feel proud of Shylock when viewed in context.

Let's try to view *The Merchant of Venice* with a liberal perspective and excuse any uncomfortable aspects of the writing for being cornered within the confines and strictures of the times.

The trajectory of *The Merchant of Venice* is made clear in its long title:

> "The most excellent Historie of the Merchant of Venice. With the extreame Crueltie of Shylocke the Jewe towards the sayd Merchant, in cutting a just pound of his flesh: and the obtaining of Portia by the choyse of three chests."

Shylock is cruel; though his legal demand for retribution is "just". Shylock is made more militant, more fundamentalist in his faith as a result of his perceived maltreatment by Christian capitalists. If he turns as vile in his cruelty as his persecutors, then they only have their own example to blame:

> "If a Jew wrong a Christian, what is humility? Revenge! If a Christian wrong a Jew, what should his sufferance be by Christian example? – why revenge! The villainy you teach me I will execute." (IIIi)

Horatio

MEMO

January 2nd '97

From: Luke Strong, Artistic Director

To: Horatio J. Dowden-Adams, Dramaturg

Re: THE MERCHANT OF VENICE

Horatio – am I dirty-minded, or are the body puns Shakespeare uses throughout the play saucy, pornographic, erotic? Is Shylock smirking knowingly (homophobically?) when he demands of Antonio the forfeiture of:

"   An equal pound
Of your fair flesh, to be cut off and taken
In what part of your body pleaseth me" (Iiii) –

implicitly the uncircumcised Christian penis of the gay man, no? (I take it Antonio is gay.)

The play ends with Gratianio's graphic, earthy pun to Nerissa, who is still in disguise wearing her trappings as a boy. The pun is on the anus/vagina of "ring":

"Well, while I live, I'll fear no other thing
So sore, as keeping safe Nerissa's ring." (V)

This couplet closes the play! What tone is Shakespeare trying to leave ringing (oops) in our ears?

I suppose that this heady brew of sex, lust for cash, terror of the Outsider channelled into racist aggression, are all the ingredients of a hit!

Luke

MEMO

January 12th '97

From: Luke Strong, Artistic Director

To: Horatio J. Dowden-Adams, Dramaturg

Re: THE MERCHANT OF VENICE

Horatio – Please can you get Shakespeare to cut all the Launcelot Gobbo stuff, especially with his Dad Old Gobbo?

And ask him to go easy on the Salads – the indistinguishable, wet-lettuce hangers-on Salerio and Solanio (or is it Solario and Salenio?)

And how do we make all these characters' collisions not seem totally random? Portia and Shylock only collide coincidentally after the laborious casket-choosing sequence in Portia's haven at Belmont: "All that glisters is not gold" (IIvii). Pah! A cliché! Even when Bassanio has eventually made his leaden choice (as late as IIIii – get on with it!) Shakespeare then has to motor the story along. How does he do it? By delivering a letter from Antonio bearing a far too important plot development to have relied on the Italian postal system, that's how! It's as if the plodding craftsman can't keep up with the speed of the imaginative story-teller. When he did this with the Friar's tardy correspondence in *Romeo & Juliet* we ached in anticipation of the tragic consequences. Here we just don't buy it. Shakespeare almost acknowledges his laziness when Portia produces yet another (dis)missive at the end of the play:

"You shall not know by what strange accident
I chanced on this letter…" (V)

Pull the other one, says weary Antonio, "I am dumb!" (V). Dumb-founded. Dumb as in stupid not to question such a clumsy bit of plotting. And dumb as in won't say a word because it's nearly the end of the play and we'd all like to go home please.

Luke

MEMO

January 24th '97

From: Horatio J. Dowden-Adams, Dramaturg

To: Luke Strong, Artistic Director

Re: MERCHANT

Luke – don't you think that sometimes it's good that Shakespeare doesn't slow up to smooth out the wrinkles, but just keeps ploughing on? Clumsy Portia's revelation may be, but it'll be effective in performance, I think.

Horatio

◇◇◇

MEMO

January 25th '97

From: Luke Strong, Artistic Director

To: Horatio J. Dowden-Adams

Re: THE MERCHANT OF VENICE

H – so what's going on in the courtroom scene? It relies upon a disguised, duplicitous Portia aping legal technicalities to save Antonio. She is disgracefully vindictive towards Shylock, robbing him of fortune and faith in a travesty of justice (IVi). It's cynical.

The whole play feels like a rush job to me, getting it out of the way after *Richard II* because he's on a roll and wants to get on with *Henry IV*. The dénouement involving the hastily planted prop of the ring (enough said about that lewd signifier) certainly suggests haste.

Why couldn't he allow a little more daylight into the murk and mist and gloom? The play's setting is more akin to Elizabethan Bankside and Shoreditch than the glorious Piazza San Marco and the Canal Grande of Venice. Into these back passages (you see, he's got me at it now!) scurry the yapping Christians and the arrogant Jew.

L.

◇◇

January 7th '97

Dear William,

THE MERCHANT OF VENICE

Sorry it has taken a while to get back to you about *The Merchant of Venice.*

Antonio's merchant ventures are *de rigueur* in the context of Elizabethan conquistadors like Drake and Raleigh. And your sources are honourable, and not just European, but Persian and Indian too.

I note you've dipped into fellow dramatist Anthony Munday's 1580 story *Zelauto or The Fountain of Fame.* And you owe a lot to Marlowe: you've taken the story of Barabas' daughter Abigail's conversion to Christianity from his 1589 play *The Jew of Malta* and used it as a prompt for Shylock's daughter, Jessica, for example.

In short, the play is an impressive pedigree mongrel. And we'd like to pursue it.

Yours,

Horatio J. Dowden-Adams

Dramaturg

January 29th '97

Dear William,

THE MERCHANT OF VENICE

I know that your own father, John, was found guilty of usury when you were just six years old. And that new sonnet you've sent me talks of a "Profitless usurer" (4).

Thinking about your lack of sympathy for usurers, it dawns on me that *The Merchant of Venice* is an attack on usuring *fathers* and not Jews. Your father was a socially respectable local man, an alderman no less, who became embarrassing to your childhood self by his bankruptcy and loss of local influence. You certainly weren't going to follow such a father, who had let you down, into the family trade of glove-making. (I don't think any of your siblings have either, although I hear your brother Gilbert is a haberdasher in the West Midlands.)

So, you reject your father and all he stood for by veering to the opposite extreme domestically and professionally – Jessica-like in your rejection of the very fundamentals, leaving his closet Catholicism and his conservative hometown for the multi-faith, creative crucible of unrespectable but profitable London, where no-one need judge you by your forefathers but just you for who you are.

The Merchant of Venice is a punishment for your father, your letter of rejection to him.

Much love,

Luke Strong

Artistic Director

MEMO

February 3rd '97

From: Horatio Dowden-Adams

To: Luke Strong

Re: HENRY IV PART ONE

Luke –

Fathers and sons.

Shakespeare had Bolingbroke in *Richard II* delivering a great teaser about his son, Hal, heralding the forthcoming *Henry IV* plays:

> "Enquire at London 'mongst the taverns there,
> For there they say he doth frequent
> With unrestrainèd loose companions,
> Even such, they say, as stand in narrow lanes
> And beat our watch and rob our passengers,
> Whilst he, young, wanton and effeminate boy,
> Takes on the point of honour to support
> So dissolute a crew." (*Richard II*, Viii)

Eastcheap: the cradle of Hal's adolescence.

There's something of Shakespeare in Henry, I think. Henry's disappointment is kingly – but there's also guilt at not being the best of fathers, of being out of touch with his son:

> "Could such inordinate and low desires,
> Such poor, such bare, such lewd, such mean attempts,
> Such barren pleasures, rude society
> As thou art matched withal, and grafted to,
> Accompany the greatness of thy blood?"
>
> (*Henry IV Part 1*, IIIii)

This sounds like many an angry father reprimanding his children. We overstate our case, and always regret it: Henry calls Hal "degenerate." (IIIii) Hal bites his tongue, until the very next scene (IIIiii), when Hal lets off steam by playing the reproachful father-figure to Falstaff. It's ingenious.

Where Richard II was contrasted with Bolingbroke (Henry IV), now Hal is contrasted with Harry Hotspur, to the former's seeming disfavour:

"   I, by looking on the praise of him,
See riot and dishonour stain the brow
Of my young Harry." (Ii)

But Henry IV's perspective on Harry Hotspur isn't one we're encouraged to share for long. Hotspur is, as his nickname signifies, hot-headed and a bit of a prick, and is lampooned by Hal as such:

"I am not yet of Percy's mind, the Hotspur of the north, he that kills me some six or seven dozen of Scots at a breakfast, washes his hands, and says to his wife, 'Fie, upon this quiet life, I want work.'" (IIiv)

Shakespeare has taken the historical Hotspur – who was two years *Bolingbroke's senior* – and set him up in *Richard II* as a future mirror for Hal. He has also given him his "adopted name of privilege" (Vii), 'Hotspur' (that the actual Harry Percy earned for border skirmishes with the Scots) and has fun with its meaning. Even Hotspur's own father, Northumberland, scolds him as "a wasp-stung and impatient fool", self-opinionated:

"Tying thine ear to no tongue but thine own!" (Iiii)

Hotspur bristles with enthusiasm, but he's disorganised in his political rebellion against the King:

"   A plague upon it!
I have forgot the map." (IIIi)

By contrast, in Hal's adolescent rebellion against his father (there's something of Shakespeare the son in Hal too) he shows him experiencing Falstaff's "vocation" of thievery and dissipation to be sure, but also absorbing Falstaff's full-blown humanity. It's as if Shakespeare is saying that life is a series of mistakes to be learnt from; and that Falstaff's life, warts and all, has a sensibility to which we could all aspire; that we should learn to live a little. In the extraordinary play-acting scene (IIiv), where Falstaff and Hal both play both Henry IV and Hal, we get to a truth through the role-playing which makes us shudder:

FALSTAFF   (As Hal) Banish not him thy Harry's company. Banish not him thy Harry's company. Banish plump Jack, and banish all the world.

HAL   (As Henry IV) I do. I will.   (IIiv)

The repetition of "Banish not him thy Harry's company" is brilliant – even if it is a typo!

I'm not sure I can ever grow to like Hal. He's a fine psychological study in youth, to be sure, and will prove rewarding for young actors learning their craft. But as a character, he's not so appealing away from Falstaff.

Falstaff without Hal, however, is always fascinating. When Hal isn't there to be his audience, he maintains his quick-witted banter by sharing it with us, direct. And, while Shakespeare has proved himself hitherto to be such a fine writer of blank verse, Falstaff is a master of prose – a world away from those doggerel-delivering clowns.

There's something unconditional in Falstaff's love for Hal – although it can also seem parasitic, Falstaff dependent on Hal's patronage as well as his camaraderie:

"I have foresworn his company hourly any time this two and twenty years, and yet I am bewitched with the rogue's company. If the rascal have not given me medicines to make me love him, I'll be hanged." (IIii)

There's also a tension between the lovable rogue and the callous profiteer. It's all that flawed character complexity that is so richly satisfying for an audience and for the performer. And whets the appetite for *Part Two*.

Horatio

◇◇

July 16th '97

Dear William,

It's a huge shock that Ben Jonson has gone to Marshalsea prison and been tortured over his controversial play **The Isle of Dogs** for the new Pembroke's Men at the new Swan Theatre on Bankside. He was doing Thomas Nashe a favour by writing up the plot. But Nashe and the other co-writers have fled, to East Anglia.

I'm not convinced that Elizabeth will follow through her order for the playhouses to "be plucked down", but we'll have to be careful about exploring too much politics in our plays while the theatres remain forcibly closed. I'm glad you're taking up the new commission – a royal commission, no less! – while this blows over. The Falstaff follow-up **The Merry Wives of Windsor** is a safe bet in the current climate. Best not to inflame the powers that be with **Henry IV Part 2** just yet …

All the best,

Lionel Farthing

Executive Producer

Memorandum

August 9th '97

To: Luke Strong, Artistic Director

From: Horatio J. Dowden-Adams, Dramaturg

cc Sasha Radish, Producer

Re: MERRY WIVES OF WINDSOR, Shakespeare

Luke –

I enclose Shakespeare's new play which I'd be grateful if you could look at.

In my view, our company – indeed the whole of English theatre – should be aspiring in its new work beyond the predictability of plot, of the comfort-zone of the characters he displays here.

Falstaff is but a shadow of what he was in *Henry IV Part 1*; and not what we're anticipating when Shakespeare delivers *Part 2*. As for Falstaff's cronies, Mistress Quickly, Bardolph and Nim are all there, as are Pistol and Justice Shallow who are going to pop up in *Henry IV Part 2*. Otherwise the new characters are:

- <u>racist</u> – a garrulous Welsh priest; a ridiculous French doctor
- <u>ageist</u> – simpering young lovers; knackered old lechers
- <u>sexist</u> – the bourgeois, tittle-tattling Merry Wives themselves.

On the plus side? Not much in my view. There is pathos and venom in the treatment of the jealous character of Ford. Otherwise I get the impression that this is a mid-life crisis play in which a former radical has lost his balls (the dramatist, as well as his protagonist). There is a witty turn of phrase or two, and occasionally his perceptive eye roves; but too often the eye is misty, and the phrases turned just aren't sharp enough.

There's also an unforgivably tedious, lewd, Latin-learning schoolroom scene, full of quibbling, with a self-indulgent self-portrait of a hapless schoolboy called William (IVi).

What's more, so much of the play is in prosaic prose that you wonder if Shakespeare's lost the appetite for verse altogether.

What's shocking is that *The Merry Wives of Windsor* is pretty much wholly original, like *Love's Labour's Lost*: which, if I'm honest, doesn't say much for his thinking on his own, does it?

Before we reject it outright, however, I suppose we need to ask ourselves:

1. will it take a leap beyond its complacency if Shakespeare is pushed?

2. is this benign middle-brow theatre, set in a provincial backwater, really the stuff for our audiences? (Please don't say yes.)

3. should we try it out on tour before bringing it into town, to see if it has legs?

If I'm honest, I don't think it's salvageable. I'm not surprised, given that he dashed it off in a fortnight, apparently. Next time, let's think twice before being flattered into hastily commissioning a flimsy off-shoot to a meaty political drama at the behest of our conservative royal patron.

Horatio

Memo

August 10th '97

From: Luke Strong, Artistic Director

To: Horatio J. Dowden-Adams, Dramaturg

cc: Sasha Radish, Producer

Re: MERRY WIVES OF WINDSOR, Shakespeare

Horatio –

I don't think you're giving it its due at all. Of course it's not *Henry IV Part 1*, and of course Falstaff isn't the same kind of *tour de force* he was in that magnificent play. But trust me, it will run and run and be twice as popular as *Henry IV* in performance.

It's a light comedy, for heaven's sake! Shakespeare has successfully taken a popular character and thought laterally. Sure, the Witch of Brentford stuff is silly (IVii), as are the stag horns (Vv) and the rest of it *on the page*. But believe you me, it will go down a treat on stage. The scene with the identical letters is breathtakingly clever. As is the final scene in the woods (Vv) – antlers notwithstanding. If the language isn't as good as *Henry IV Part 1* – or isn't as dazzling as in his previous comedies – then that's beside the point. The play doesn't exist for that reason. That's not why it was commissioned. It's unashamed entertainment and will open a flurry of new doors onto the bourgeois, boulevard genre of sexual farce. We should programme it.

And don't be such a snob! "Middle-brow" people need their fun too!

Luke

August 15th '97

Luke, Horatio –

It does strike me that *Merry Wives* might make a good operetta.

Sasha

<><><><><><><><><><><><><><><><><><><><><><><><><><><><><><><><><><><>

MEMO

October 7th '97

From: Horatio

To: Luke

Re: HIV Pt 2

Henry IV Part 1 displayed a new maturity. *Part 2* has reached even higher levels of new-found wisdom and sophistication. Perhaps it's because Shakespeare's rooted it less in his source material and more in his own life? Those magnificent scenes in Gloucestershire between Falstaff and Justices Shallow and Silence must have been informed by watching his father, as Justice of the Peace for Stratford-upon-Avon, co-ordinating the rounding-up of militia men. The scene recruiting Mouldy, Wart, Feeble, Bullcalf and Shadow is both hilarious and chilling. (I'd hazard that Francis Feeble the Tailor is based on Shakespeare's Warwickshire haberdasher brother Gilbert.)

Hal banishing Falstaff, "on pain of death" (Vv) after his coronation as Henry V, is devastating. Children need an adult mentor to look up to, in whom to confide, who isn't their parent – which is part of the reason we have the custom of appointing (fairy) godparents. But to reject that surrogate parent –

"The tutor and feeder of my riots" (Vv) –

in such a publicly humiliating way is astonishing. This next stage in Hal's maturation, a rite of passage to reject his surrogate father now that he's buried his natural father, is cold-hearted. Hal does claim to have replaced both these father figures with his former enemy, the Lord Chief Justice:

"You shall be as a father to my youth" (Vii).

But this is surely said for political expediency?

This is a coming-of-age play – for its author, as much as for its characters.

Horatio

◇◇◇

December 12th '97

Dear William

HENRY IV

I have just taken my teenage daughter to see *Henry IV Parts 1 & 2*. I was moved – especially by *Part 2* which has moments of deep reflection compared to the more brassy *Part 1* (*pace* the play-acting scene (*Part 1*, IIiv)). And she was impressed too.

But as I watched, I wondered what was really in it for her? This play about squabbling men, battling it out in tit-for-tat boys' games. This play about fathers and sons and their surrogates. She's a daughter on the verge of womanhood, consciously European in a globalising world. She disdains the bloody mess that millennia of male civil war and politics (same thing, really) have got us into. You do offer her the feisty Kate, threatening to break her husband Hotspur's little finger if he doesn't tell her why he hasn't slept with her for a fortnight (*Part 1*, IIiii). (She has something of her namesake's spirit from *The Taming of the Shrew*.) But otherwise the best you offer my daughter as a role model is Doll Tearsheet! And no Mums!

88

Write a play with your young female audience in mind! Write a play about Boudicca!

Lecture over!

Best wishes,

Sasha Radish

Producer

◇◇

Luke Strong's Diary

September 17th '98

MUCH ADO ABOUT NOTHING

The greatest achievement of *Love's Labour's Lost* is *Much Ado About Nothing*. And I don't mean to damn with faint praise! Beatrice and Benedick are born of their prototypes Berowne and Rosaline:

BEROWNE   Did not I dance with you in Brabant once?

ROSALINE   Did not *I* dance with *you* in Brabant once?

BEROWNE   I know you did.

ROSALINE   How needless was it then to ask the question!
                                                                    (*LLL*, II)

Here they are again, only their childishness has grown up:

BEATRICE   I wonder that you will be talking, Signior
             Benedick: nobody marks you.

BENEDICK   What, my dear Lady Disdain! Are you yet living?
                                                          (*Much Ado*, Ii)

This is the banter of those who appear to scorn love actually craving it the most.

Where Berowne and Rosaline resort to self-conscious poetry, Benedick and Beatrice talk chiefly in prose. And what prose!

Within its unforced wit, there is an ease. It is rhythmically vivacious, active. When Benedick resorts to the conventional poetry of love, he's useless:

"   *The god of love,*
       That sits above
And knows me, and knows me,
       How pitiful I deserve –

… Marry, I cannot show it in rhyme; I have tried. I can find out no rhyme to 'lady' but 'baby' – an innocent rhyme; for 'scorn', 'horn' – a hard rhyme; for 'school', 'fool' – a babbling rhyme; very ominous endings! No, I was not born under a rhyming planet…" (Vii)

In exposing his inadequacies as a poetic lover, he reveals himself to be a consummate master of prose. Up until *Henry IV*, I was under the impression that Shakespeare must dream in the iambic pentameters of his blank verse. With Falstaff, he demonstrated how inventive and yet at ease he is with prose. Benedick is Falstaff's heir. Beatrice is no less begot by Falstaff.

What's astonishing about Beatrice and Benedict is that, strictly speaking, they are merely the sub-plot! Their sparring and eventual love-match shouldn't be leading, but playing second-fiddle to the gross deception and gullibility within the Claudio-Hero love story. But it doesn't; it uses similar tools to steal the show.

So when Benedick is up a tree hearing a planted conversation about what he is surprised to learn, but is ready to believe – Beatrice's love for him – he mis-interprets all subsequent exchanges and signals:

BENEDICK   Here comes Beatrice. By this day, she's a fair lady! I do spy some marks of love in her.

BEATRICE   Against my will I am sent to bid you come into dinner…

BENEDICK   … Ha! 'Against my will I am sent to bid you
              come into dinner' – there's a double meaning in
              that. (IIiii)

In the next, parallel scene, Beatrice falls into a similar trap, and
uncharacteristically expresses herself in rhyming, tum-te-tum
love poetry, which is startling after all her muscley prose:

"   And, Benedick, love on, I will requite thee,
Taming my wild heart to thy loving hand.
If thou dost love, my kindness shall incite thee
To bind our loves up in a holy band…" (IIIi)

She couldn't top Benedick – he'd said it all in the scene before
her – and Shakespeare never repeats himself. So he tries
something else – not quite as brilliant as Benedick's prose,
perhaps, but at least it's different.

Shakespeare's really audacious when he chooses the most
emotionally heated moment in the play to have Benedick
attempt to woo Beatrice in their tentative first love scene
together! In the aftershock of Hero being jilted at the altar, and
the Friar keeping up the impression that she died of grief, no
less, it couldn't be bolder:

BENEDICK   Come, bid me do anything for thee.

BEATRICE   Kill Claudio!

BENEDICK   Ha! Not for the wide world.   (IVi)

Beatrice challenges Benedick further:

"I would eat his heart in the market-place!… O that I were
a man for his sake, or that I had any friend would be a man
for my sake! But manhood is melted into curtsies, valour
into compliment, and men are only turned into tongue, and
trim ones too…" (IVi)

I love the way Shakespeare subverts the mood of the play
throughout with uncomfortable moments like this, right up to
the very end. In the midst of the weddings and resolutions – the

conventional conclusions to a good comedy – a messenger dashes on (presumably the same guy as at the beginning of the play, in which case it's a masterstroke) to let the assembled company know that the evil Don

"   John is ta'en flight
    And brought with armed men back to Messina." (Viv)

To which Benedick, not wishing to spoil a good party, answers with a dismissive Mediterranean '*mañana*':

    "Think not on him till tomorrow. I'll devise thee brave
    punishments for him. Strike up, pipers!" (Viv)

And then they dance.

With this play I think Shakespeare may spawn a whole new, independent comic tradition in the romantic comedy or rom-com. This play is different from his other comedies: more mature, more sure-footed. It has a different texture. He is a true innovator.

<><><><><><><><><><><><><><><><><><><><><><><><><><><><><><><><><><><><>

September 18th '98

Dear William,

MUCH ADO

I'm intrigued by the clown-Constable Dogberry, despite his malapropisms – "Comparisons are odorous" (IIIv) – and his asinine repetition:

    "Do not forget to specify, when time and place shall serve,
    that I am an ass." (Vi)

He is the moral police of this society. And the plot police of your play. So, if he also mangles his words, then it's because of his dedication to the job in hand, trying to be precise and methodical in a world of upper class wits, no?

Best,

Luke

◇◇◇

MEMO

September 21st '98

From: Luke, AD

To: Horatio, LM

Re: MUCH ADO ABOUT NOTHING

The title is deceptively simple and seemingly dismissive. Much Ado About Not(h)ing, as Elizabethan performers might pronounce it, is observing and spying that thinks it has seen truth but has actually seen or misinterpreted a distorted, misleading picture.

And the "nothing" is actually not nothing at all, but a big deal – the false accusation of whoring made against Hero – and therefore it's not a question of mountains being made out of molehills so much as misunderstandings and misapprehensions causing mayhem.

There's also the sexual pun of no thing, no penis, a pudenda. Incidentally, is that why he's called Bene–*dick* and not Bene–dict (as in Christian benediction)? Or is Shakespeare just making Benedick more grounded, one of the soldier-lads, like Tom, Dick, or Harry?

Luke

September 23rd '98

Dear Mr Shakespeare,

Ben Jonson will avoid hanging for killing his fellow actor Gabriel Spencer in a duel in Hoxton Fields a couple of days ago. Although he's been imprisoned before, this counts as a first offence, and thus he can claim Benefit of Clergy because he knows Latin. His thumb will, however, be branded. He will, in more senses than one, be a marked man.

Yours,

Clerk of Clerkenwell

◇◇

December 8th '98

Dear William,

MUCEDORUS

I'm thinking of reviving the old pot-boiler, the guaranteed box office pastoral comedy Mucedorus. If you had a hand in writing Mucedorus at the beginning of the '90s, as rumour has it, then you'll be chuffed. And in Mucedorus, it's great having a role for an actual bear! You could use that again one day.

Best wishes,

Lionel Farthing

Executive Producer

December 13th '98

Dear William,

THE ILIAD

I see your fellow playwright George Chapman published his translation of the first seven parts of Homer's *The Iliad* earlier this year. You mentioned "Troilus the first employer of pandars" in *Much Ado* (Vii). Have you ever thought of writing a Greek drama? Or are you too immersed in the Romans and the Stoics?

Best wishes,

Horatio J. Dowden-Adams

Dramaturg

◇◇

December 31st '98

Dear Mr Shakespeare,

You have arrived! Love's Labour's Lost, Richard III and Richard II all published this year – with your name, at last, on the cover! But don't let it go to your head: it's still the actors, not the playwrights, who get star-billing on the playbills...
A. Thespian

◇◇

January 1st '99

Dear William,

I think that Will Kemp's departure from the Lord Chamberlain's Men as you all move into the Globe will give the acting company – and your plays – a new lease of life. Kemp has been fun – Launce, Gobbo, Dogberry – but more of a clown, a natural fool, than a man of wit. Which is why

95

you gave the more challenging role of Falstaff to Thomas Pope.

With Kemp gone, you are freed from spending the rest of your career finding cheap gags for comic turns.

Welcome your new fool Robert Armin as an intellectual. He's recently completed the manuscript for his study of fooling: *Fool Upon Fool*. I think the transition from Kemp to Armin will be like the move from the old Theatre in Shoreditch to the new Globe on Bankside: The Theatre, as its name suggests, was efficient and functional; The Globe carries far greater symbolic significance.

Shoreditch's loss is Bankside's gain. The Hoxton locals will miss The Theatre's contribution to the poor of the parish, but at least their ears will be relieved of you all literally drumming up an audience.

I believe 1599 is going to be a watershed in your career.

All the best,

Sasha Radish

Producer

P.S. Kemp's going to Morris dance his way to Norwich – a Nine-Day-Wonder; the stuff of legends; 'Kemp's Jig' the balladeers will call it.

◇◇

February 2nd '99

Dear William,

THE PASSIONATE PILGRIM

I don't understand why the printer William Jaggard has claimed all the poems in *The Passionate Pilgrim* are by you, when it includes just two of your sonnets? My guess is that he thinks your name on the cover is a sign of popularity. And quality.

Best wishes,

Manfred Mild
Editorial Director

March 3rd '99

Dear William,

ARDEN FARCE

> "   All the world's a stage
> And all the men and women merely players…" (*AYLI* IIvii)

A perfect sentiment for your new world at the Globe! And I love the fact you're using it as your Latin motto on the flag fluttering above your new theatre: "*Totus Mundus Agit Histrionem*".

I have to confess I did wonder what you were up to with such a retrograde form – a Pastoral, emulating Lyly's plays – in this new comedy *As You Like It*. And I thought it possibly a cheap shot of one-upmanship to cash in on the popularity of Anthony Munday's Robin Hood plays with the Admiral's Men at Henslowe's Rose last year – *The Downfall of Robert, Earl of Sherwood* and *The Death of Robert* etc. (dreadful titles). But when we realise that we're not in some eternal spring-summer, but in a harsh, "desert city" (IIi), and everyone, being a courtier, is ill-equipped to cope, you take us to a new place.

After such high hopes, Rosalind's

> "Well, this is the Forest of Arden!" (IIiv)

sounds ambiguous, to say the least – as Touchstone's response unequivocally isn't:

> "Ay, now am I in Arden, the more fool I." (IIiv)

97

(Is this is spoken from the heart, William, echoing your sentiments on each of your rare returns from the buzz of metropolitan London to the somnolence of provincial Stratford on the edge of the actual Forest of Arden? The play is nominally set in France, like your other comedies hitherto have been set in Italy – it's just that you seem to give up the pretence even more quickly than usual!)

As You Like It is a relief after *Love's Labour's Lost*, if I'm honest! Although you are incorrigibly playing a similar game of literary clever-cleverness, alluding to, and often satirising contemporary taste in the niceties of poetry. But you're not parading quite the same level of impenetrable in-jokes for educated toffs. You're making the humour more accessible. I like it when the simple country folk seem to have the last laugh over the sophisticated townies, like Corin the shepherd:

> "The property of rain is to wet and fire to burn; that good pasture makes fat sheep; and that a great cause of the night is lack of the sun; that he that hath learned no wit by nature nor art, may complain of good breeding – or comes from a very dull kindred."   (IIIii)

Touchstone mocks Corin as a "natural philosopher" (IIIii), his meaning of "natural" being foolish; but, to me, Corin's naturalness seems more appealing than the artifice of Touchstone.

Touchstone touches upon the dangers of the courtly, city wit of the poet:

> "When a man's verses can not be understood, nor a man's good wit seconded with the forward child, understanding, it strikes a man more dead than a great reckoning in a little room." (IIIiii)

"Ye reckoning" is how the official papers dubbed the fatal stabbing of Marlowe in that room above the inn in Deptford back in May '93. You're still haunted by it, aren't you? Was he accidentally wounded in an argument over the bill? Over his sexual preferences? Notorious atheism? Was he killed in a fit of jealousy for his fine poetry, or contemptuously killed for his bad verses? Was it a politically-motivated assassination because of his alleged spying activities?

Who knows?

With many of your fellow writers now having their books publicly burned because of the Bishop's Ban, and being thrown into prison for incitement to insurrection, you're well aware how precarious the life of a poet-playwright can be. You pay great respect to Marlowe in your homage to the impression of great wealth of Marlowe's Jew of Malta, Barabas:

"Infinite riches in a little room." (*Jew of Malta*, Ii)

Marlowe also wrote the epic poem *Hero and Leander* where Jupiter has a thing for the cross-dressing boy-lover Ganymede, an inspiration for *As You Like It*.

Marlowe was your exact contemporary. You were both born in 1564 in the country (he in Kent; you in Warwickshire). By 1593, you both had written a similar number of plays each. His was the defining voice of Henslowe's Rose. I wonder what greater plays he would have gone on to write – you too, perhaps, with Kit as your spur.

I'm sorry, but not surprised to see you still aching for the loss of Marlowe. If only as a competitor rather than as a friend.

Yours,

Luke Strong

Artistic Director

March 7th '99

Dear William,

AS YOU LIKE IT

I see you're tapping into the fashion for melancholia with Jacques. But it seems a genuine condition in him rather than the kind of affectation Ben Jonson satirised in *Everyman in His Humour* last year.

Now, cuts. Plot set-up, usually your strong point, isn't so hot here, I'm afraid. Orlando explains his predicament to a man who already knows the score:

> "As I remember, Adam, it was upon this fashion bequeath'd me by will but poor a thousand crowns, on his blessing, and, *as thou say'st*, charged my brother…" etc. (Ii)

Then giving Charles all the back-story, about the banished and usurping Duke brothers, won't wash. Charles is a wrestler! All brawn and no brain. Trust me, we will pick things up really quickly. So be brave and cut the first scene altogether.

Then at the risk of upsetting your idiosyncratic lop-sidedness and the intangible essence of your play, I'm going to suggest radically restructuring the first part of the play as follows:

Pre-show	Charles already wrestling – elements of Iii
Ii	Cut
Iii	introducing Celia/Rosalind/Touchstone + Orlando
Iiii	banishment of Rosalind
IIi	Cut
IIii	Cut
IIiii	Orlando/Adam – trim and incorporate elements of Ii here as necessary
IIiv	arrival of Celia/Ros/Touchstone in Arden; introducing the shepherds

| IIv | introducing Jacques and the exiled court – incorporate elements of IIi |
| IIvi | Adam can go no further (NB use some of IIiii here?) |

then play out as in draft

I hope you'll agree that this will power the story along. With all due respect, I think it needs it.

Best wishes,

Horatio J. Dowden-Adams

Dramaturg

◇◇

March 18th '99

Dear Mr Shakespeare,

AS YOU LIKE IT

Your sexual politics are intriguing. The relationship between Orlando and Rosalind is erotic – Rosalind, a boy-actor playing the young woman character, Rosalind, who plays a young boy, 'Ganymede', who plays a young woman, 'Rosalind'...

To chaperone them, you have the mischievous, manicured, feminine companion Celia. She's sharp, conscious of the narrative she's in. She is ever-present, saying little, observing the action critically, as our Chorus. What little she does say is often uncomfortable. Play-acting as the priest in the mock wedding of Rosalind's Ganymede to Orlando, she stumbles:

"I can not say the words." (IVi)

She then chastises Rosalind:

"You have simply misused our sex in your love-prate. We must have your doublet and hose plucked over your head and show the world what the bird hath done to her own nest." (IVi)

Rosalind takes the initiative in her authoritative male disguise, but it is also the obstacle to her love-union with Orlando. Her emotions get confused in her 'pretend' wooing of Orlando because there is true self-discovery in this process of artificial courtship. Orlando says:

"O, how bitter a thing it is to look into happiness through another man's eyes." (Vii)

He could be speaking on Rosalind's behalf too.

Rosalind – having been the director of proceedings, over and above and outside the world of the play – has to disappear off stage at the crucial moment, to put on a frock. You get round this with characteristic artistic licence, employing one of your *deus ex machinas*: Hymen, god of marriage, pops on to do a masque. And you, the author, also help out your character when she needs it:

"   His uncle,
Whom he reports to be a great magician,
Obscured in the circle of this forest" (Viv).

You are Rosalind's "old religious uncle" (IIIii), the "old religious man" that Jacques de Boys ("second son of old Sir Rowland") says he's met when he turns up at the end out of the blue (Viv).

Yours sincerely,

Professor Rosita Sanchez

Graduate Gender Studies

May 8th '99

Dear Luke,

HENRY V

For my forthcoming lecture series on Access or Excess in the Socio-Political Dichotomies of International Aggression in the History Plays Sagas of William Shakespeare, I'm trying to get a handle on Shakespeare's attitude to patriotism, but, as ever, I'm finding he is equivocal! Which, as far as the for-or-against, black-and-white polarisations of patriotism are concerned, would make him a sceptic, to say the least!

Henry IV's advice to Hal at the end of *Henry IV Part 2*, to pursue a domestic strategy of distraction through foreign policy aggression, is pragmatic, given what he's been through:

" Busy giddy minds
With foreign quarrels." (*HIV2*, IVv)

So Hal, now Henry V, pursues his dodgy claim to the French crown via a convoluted 60+ lines of spurious Salic law (inheritance through the female line). It's so long-winded that even Henry impatiently questions the Archbishop of Canterbury's Holinshed-quoting explanation:

"May I with right and conscience make this claim?" (*HV* Iii)

Then, to provoke France into battle, he sends the impetuous Dauphin a ton of tennis-balls. Job done. All-out war ensues.

(Actually, why does the Archbishop of Canterbury keep going on and on (Iii)? Isn't there a danger of losing the audience so near the top of the show? And/or is Shakespeare expecting you to cut it as you see fit? Or does he want you to play it for laughs, Hal clock-watching etc.?)

We weren't sure whether to like Hal by the end of *Henry IV Part 2*. He's now going to be as ruthless in his pursuit of power as he was with biding his time, avoiding his father, and (ab)using his friends in Eastcheap. He is the scourge of Falstaff:

"The king has killed his heart" (*HV* IIi),

laments Mistress Quickly as Falstaff dies off-stage. And later, Henry does nothing to prevent the hanging of Bardolph for stealing from the battlefield. It's all very slippery, because Henry V balances Machiavellianism with jingoism.

So for all the surface patriotism in the seductive power of his rhetoric –

"Once more unto the breach, dear friends, once more!"
(IIIi) –

and the stirring affectation of his Saint Crispin's Day dedication of the Battle of Agincourt –

"We few, we happy few, we band of brothers…" (IViii) –

we actually shudder at the cold, calculation of the new, young man:

"Every soldier kill his prisoners" (IVvi),

he commands before the last battle against the French.

When Henry beats the besieged citizens of Harfleur into submission through monstrous threats to unleash his soldiers, "rough and hard of heart," we are appalled. He says they will mow,

    "   like grass
    Your fresh-fair virgins and your flow'ring infants…
    What is't to me, when you yourselves are cause,
    If your pure maidens fall into the hand
    Of hot and forcing violation?…
                          … look to see
    The blind and bloody soldier with foul hand
    Defile the locks of your shrill-shrieking daughters,
    Your fathers taken by the silver beards
    And their most reverend heads dashed to the walls,
    Your naked infants spitted upon pikes…" (IIIiii)

And so he goes on, the pathological psychopath. Is this threat justifiable in the name of patriotism?

But we can not reject Henry, however repugnant we find him, because Shakespeare casts him in our own image. We are complicit in his re-enactment of this story, because of Shakespeare's greatest innovation in this play: the Chorus (not an ensemble as in a Greek drama, but a solo turn. Economics? A virtue of necessity?)

The Chorus constantly seeks our "pardon", saying that the theatre is "unworthy", inadequate to recreate the tale (Prologue). The Chorus entreats us to:

> "Piece out the imperfections with our thoughts" (Prologue);
> "And eke out our performance with your mind" (III),

in

> "The quick forge and working-house of thought." (V)

It's almost as if Shakespeare's own sense of stagecraft is embarrassed, with hindsight, by his previous History Plays and/or by the productions they have received to date – I'm thinking particularly of the *Henry VI* plays. The Chorus is a show-off apologist, flaunting the descriptive power of words and word-painting to excite our imagination, but an apology nonetheless. (I'm assuming Shakespeare's written the part of Chorus for himself.) Why apologise?:

> "O, for a Muse of fire!" (Prologue)

Shakespeare gets that little round "O", the "wooden O", the new spherical Gl**O**be theatre, into the very first word of the play. Genius!

Yours sincerely,

Dr Chris Cole

Faculty of Politics and Liberal Arts and Social Sciences

May 10th '99

Dear William,

Henry V is an uncomfortable play, which will serve you and the Chamberlain's Men well as your swansong to The Theatre in Shoreditch and decamp, trodden boards and all, to build The Globe on the South Bank in Southwark where **Henry V** will also inaugurate the new playhouse. It looks back, with all the echoes of The Wars of the Roses; while at the same time projecting forward with ground-breaking dramaturgy. It's a perfect moment to sign your new Globe Theatre and Chamberlain's Men contract.

Best,

Lionel Farthing

Executive Producer

◇◇◇

May 15th '99

Dear William,

HENRY V

Now that Essex and his Caesar-like efforts to crush the Irish rebellion have failed, and Elizabeth is distancing herself from him, you'll want to make a number of revisions to **Henry V**.

This is a play written in a period of change for you – creatively and financially – and in a period of cultural unease, what with the Bishop's Ban on published satires and all the public book burning that's still going on. So I really think you should lie low for a while. Don't stop working by any means, but don't draw attention to yourself. Toe the line. You've got the new cultural enterprise of the Globe to think about.

And it's probably best if you didn't publish for a while either. Your plays are safer in the new playhouse. No Bishop can burn that down.

Best wishes,

Lionel Farthing

Executive Producer

<><><><><><><><><><><><><><><><><><><><><><><><><><><><><><><><><><><><>

May 20ᵗʰ '99

Dear Mr Shakespeare,

HENRY V

You have your cake and eat it, don't you, in *Henry V*? Propagandist twaddle yet stuffed with anti-war sentiment. You are offsetting heroic aspiration with sobering reality.

When the vagabond Eastcheap army raucously sets off for France, the King of France wryly observes:

"Thus comes the English with full power upon us." (IIiv)

Henry's "Once more unto the breach" (IIIi) is parodied in Bardolph's ineffectual

"On, on, on, on, on! To the breach! To the breach!" (IIIii)

Henry is humbled by taking a stroll, in disguise, around the British encampment the night before the Battle of Agincourt –

"A little touch of Harry in the night" (Chorus, IV) –

to hear what the common soldier thinks of it all. Your soldier, Michael Williams, takes an anti-heroic view of the situation:

"All those legs and arms and heads chopped off…few die well that die in battle, for how can they charitably dispose of anything when blood is their argument?" (IVi)

Your play is undeniably barn-storming. *And* pacifist. You'd be welcome on both sides of the barricades, come the revolution.

Yours,

Dr Chris Cole

Lecturer

◇◇

June 1st '99

William –

Can we cut the leek scene (Vi)? It's not funny and does neither you, nor the Welsh, any favours.

Thank you.

Luke Strong

Artistic Director

◇◇

MEMO

July 7th '99

From: Horatio

To: Luke

Re: JULIUS CAESAR

It's strange to think, isn't it, that it is Sir Thomas North of all people who translated the French version of Plutarch's epic *Lives of the Most Noble Grecians and Romanes* that informs so much of Shakespeare's new play. North: English Captain in the Irish Wars who would make Falstaff's mode of recruiting seem positively benign!

As we all appreciated when he wrote *Henry V*, Shakespeare has to tread this fine line at the moment: between popular exploration of the opposing political ideologies in the world of Caesar's Rome, and what is going on in contemporary politics with those self-styled English Caesars: Essex; and the Queen. (She has a bust of Caesar at Greenwich palace and a tapestry at Hampton Court depicting his assassination. She's also currently translating Plutarch's *On Curiosity*. I wonder if Shakespeare knows?)

Despite being an off-shore island in Northern Europe, on the cold, dank, distant fringes of a hearty and hot Mediterranean civilization, England looks to Rome in its attempt to punch above its weight. Through education, culture, and a Spanish Armada-conquering navy, England aspires to the grandeur of the Roman Empire.

Which is why then and now discourse with each other in Shakespeare's play, merging in the dramatist's trick of using the historical past as a perspective on the present. Shakespeare has fun with this, inviting us to spot the deliberate anachronisms: chiming clocks (IIi, IIiii, IIiv); Elizabethan clothes in a land of togas; "chimney-tops" (Ii), etc.

And he seems to enjoy writing about the period of anarchic flux between one state apparatus, the Democratic Republic, and the next: New Imperialism. It's also a period where, like Jack Cade and his mob in *Henry VI Part 2*, the fickle people have an opportunity to take the power away from the ruling classes, but flunk it. They only have the lynching of a dreaming poet to show for themselves:

CINNA   I am Cinna the poet!

PLEBEIAN   Tear him for his bad verses! Tear him for his
            bad verses!

CINNA   I am not Cinna the conspirator!

PLEBEIAN   It is no matter, his name's Cinna: pluck but his
            name out of his heart. (IIIiii)

Another hapless poet turns up at Brutus and Cassius'
encampment outside Sardis with the aim of smoothing over
the discord between the conspirators. And they do unite
temporarily when they both turn on this poet, viciously
scapegoating him, lashing out at their prey:

CASSIUS   Ha, ha! How vilely doth this cynic rhyme!

BRUTUS   Get you hence, sirrah! Saucy fellow, hence!...
                 What should the wars do with these jigging
                                                    fools? (IVii)

No wonder poets are so paranoid! It goes with the job.

Horatio

<hr>

July 18th '99

Dear William,

You have carefully called your play *Julius Caesar*, which is
good marketing, big name recognition. And canny because
it will attract less attention than if you'd been seen by your
title to venerate Marcus Brutus. As ever, you wisely don't
nail your colours to the mast and declare whose side you
are on. And why should you? You're a dramatist, after all,
not a politician.

But however well *Julius Caesar* goes down in the playhouse,
I wouldn't publish it now or in the near future, if I were you.
Elizabeth's been threatened by enough conspiracies over the
course of her reign to make her inner circle think they see a
threat even where there isn't one. So putting your eulogy to
Brutus in *Antony's* mouth is shrewd:

"This was the noblest Roman of them all…
         …nature might stand up
And say to all the world: This was a man!" (Vv)

Yours,

Sasha Radish

Producer

<hr>

October 8th '99

Dear Will,

A new play for a new theatre in a new world at the dawn of a new century:

"   How many ages hence
Shall this our lofty scene be acted over,
In states unborn, and accents yet unknown?"
                    (*Julius Caesar*, IIIi)

Let's look into getting *Julius Caesar* translated for the European Theatre circuit – and any other nations and languages which may emerge in due course.

Ciao. À bientôt. Auf wiederhören.

Manfred Mild.

Publisher

<hr>

January 18th '00

Dear William,

ENGLAND'S PARNASSUS

Don't be disconsolate about your 100 entries in the commonplace quotations compilation *England's Parnassus*.

Spenser may have nearly 400, and Drayton over 200; but Spenser's dead and, for a mere playwright, you're in good company!

Best wishes,

Manfred Mild

Publisher

◇◇

January 20th '00

Dear William,

I have just seen *The True and Honourable Historie of the Life of Sir John Oldcastle, the Good Lord Cobham* in the bookshop. And your name's plastered all over the title page! Philip Henslowe's going around town saying Anthony Munday, Michael Drayton, Richard Hathaway and Robert Wilson are the real authors. With all the trouble you had with the Estate of Oldcastle, the ancestor of your illustrious Lord Chamberlain patrons, about changing the name to Falstaff, they had better watch out.

Best wishes,

Manfred Mild

Publisher

P.S. You're not related to Richard Hathaway are you? The possibility is raised in an unauthorised biography of your elusive wife. But there seem to be loads of Hathaways in Warwickshire.

February 10th '01

Dear William,

RICHARD II

We knew **Richard II** was utterly contemporary and subversive at the time it was written and first performed, five years ago now. But this potentially seditious performance of the play at the Globe, sponsored by Sir Gelly Meyrick and the other disenfranchised, malcontent supporters of the Earl of Essex, forbidden to attend court since he was released from the Tower, is going to get you into hot water.

You must already be feeling queasy that Dr John Hayward is still incarcerated for publishing the first part of his **Life and Reign of Henry IV** exactly two years ago. I know that it contained that hostage to fortune, a dedicatory eulogy to Essex, but nonetheless, everyone will have been drawing parallels between his work and your plays, Essex a Bolingbroke to Elizabeth's Richard II.

As you must know, they were trying to use the performance as populist propaganda to incite the citizens of London (well, some playgoers at least) to undermine Elizabeth (Richard II) in order to promote their man Essex (Bolingbroke) the day before his rebellion and attempted coup of February 8th. Elizabeth's no fool. She's reported to have said: "I am Richard II, know ye not that?"

Your perceived role in the controversy is bound to be questioned. Keep schtum.

Best wishes,

Lionel Farthing

Executive Producer

February 23rd '01

Dear William,

I hear you're giving a royal command performance at court tomorrow, the eve of Essex's execution.

Plays have always been feared by the political establishment as being dangerous, not because they'll necessarily incite the mob, but because they dare an audience to think, to dream. It's part of the reason theatre is so seductive – to those who are lured to work and create within it, as well as to audiences. Theatre can be a socially levelling experience. Theatre is vision and imagination and magic and transformation, rooted and grounded in bare boards and stitched frocks and practical tricks and crafted poetry.

Yet for all its liberal, laissez-faire ambience, theatre can be co-opted by the State. And, as you know, even anti-establishment mavericks find authoritarian power exciting, an aphrodisiac.

Yours,

Lionel Farthing
Executive Producer

◇◇

March 4th '01

Dear William,

SIR THOMAS MORE

Anthony Munday's in a pickle. There will be political ramifications if we don't get this one right.

A decade ago the Master of the Revels, Sir Edward Tilney, refused to give *Sir Thomas More* a licence. We're trying to get it on again now. And we need your help.

Munday is renowned as "our best plotter" (Francis Meres said as much in his *Palladis Tamia: Wits Treasury*, 1598). But his work always needs a polish. Henry Chettle's helping out (they worked together on the second play *The Death of…*in the Robin Hood two-parter) – along with young Heywood and the prolific Dekker, fellow actor-playwrights.

The scene we need help with is one in which More attempts to quell the May Day riots of 1517, when the mob were up in arms about "strangers" (foreigners, resident aliens) coming over here, stealing all our jobs, jumping housing queues, scrounging off the Health Service, living off our charity, sleeping with our women. You know the kind of thing: the scapegoating of the Other; xenophobic scaremongering. Tilney originally requested the following:

> "Leave out the insurrection wholly and the cause thereof and begin with Sir Thomas More at the mayor's sessions with a report afterwards of his good service being sheriff of London upon a mutiny against the Lombards only by short report and not otherwise at your own perils."

(Who does Tilney think he is? Government Censor, or State Dramaturg?!)

There's also another speech by More which I'd like you to take a look at, when he reflects on what it means to his intregrity now that he's been promoted yet again, this time to Lord Chancellor.

I'm hugely appreciative of your help in this matter. Even if it never gets performed, not in Elizabeth's reign at any rate, there is the principle of free speech of the artist at stake.

Many thanks.

Yours,

Luke Strong

Artistic Director

June 8th '01

Dear Mr Shakespeare,

The printer has returned your hand-written inserts for *Sir Thomas More* – which is odd, because he usually bins them or uses them for scrap. There are your usual blots and crossings out and idiosyncratic spelling and sometimes illegible handwriting – but here's the curious thing: you haven't written your name anywhere on the pages. Someone's attached a note, saying enigmatically "Hand D".

Do you want them back? Or shall we hold on to them? If so we'll send them to the archives.

Best,

Loren Spiegelei
Literary Department

◇◇◇

July 9th '01

Dear William,

THE PHOENIX AND THE TURTLE

You've nicely taken the rare, exotic, magical, Arabian bird and developed it as the symbol of all-consuming, self-sacrificing, constantly renewing love. But your poem should, of course, be called 'The Phoenix and the Turtle *Dove*'. It's not about a swimming tortoise, after all!

Best wishes,

Manfred Mild
Publisher

September 20th '01

Dear William,

I am sorry to hear about the death of your father. In my experience, as well as causing all sorts of anxieties about one's own mortality, a father's death also infantilises us. When a father passes on, we are in effect, kicked up a generation; but even if we are already fathers ourselves, our dormant childhood self is re-awakened. And if our mothers are still alive, how does it refocus our relationship with them...?

My condolences,

Bob Castle

Director

⬦⬦

October 1st '01

Dear Mr Shakespeare,

HAMLET

Let me get this straight:

Thirty years ago, Young Hamlet was born at Elsinore, the seat of Danish government – on the very day his father, Old Hamlet, King of Denmark, was away slaying Old Fortinbras, King of Norway. All Old Fortinbras' personal lands passed to the vanquishing Old Hamlet; but Old Fortinbras' brother became King of Norway. On this very same day, the Gravedigger to Elsinore was appointed as a boy apprentice.

Twenty three years ago, when Young Hamlet was seven, Yorick, the Court Jester at Elsinore, died, and was buried.

A few years ago, Young Hamlet enrolled at Wittenberg University in Germany.

117

Two months ago, Old Hamlet died. Since when, Young Fortinbras has been threatening to reclaim those lands lost by his father to Old Hamlet thirty years ago. Denmark has been put on a war footing.

A month ago, soon after Old Hamlet's funeral, his brother, Claudius, married his widow, Gertrude (Young Hamlet's mother).

Last night, guards, who keep watch at Elsinore, saw a ghost.

This morning, Claudius was elected King of Denmark by the courtiers. Young Hamlet, the only other candidate, is to be named Claudius' nominated heir, and a party is to be held in his honour tomorrow evening…

Now that's some back-story! Which is what you need for revenge drama of course. And a hero who is the very essence of existentialism.

Yours,

Loren Spiegelei

Literary Department

◇◇

MEMO

October 5th '01

From: Horatio

To: Luke

Luke – The character of Hamlet and the story of his pretend madness have been popular themes in Icelandic and Norse folklore for many centuries, long before Shakespeare reinvented it – the earliest reference comes in an 11th century

Icelandic poem, I think. Years ago I seem to remember that there was a play called *Amleth* doing the rounds. It was a classic revenge tragedy, first performed in the '80s. It was subsequently attributed to Thomas Kyd, author of the seminal Elizabethan revenge tragedy *The Spanish Tragedy*. But I think it may have been a piece of juvenilia by Will… My guess is that even if he didn't write it, he knew the play, and perceived its dramatic potential. And because it wasn't published, he had ample incentive and scope to steal the idea – from himself, or whoever. And he also knew the story would appeal to good actors, because he'd probably performed in it.

Hamlet follows the basic story of the old heroic tale quite closely, yet it departs from the spirit of the original – and from the revenge tradition – more radically and brilliantly than ever before.

Horatio

◇◇◇

MEMO

October 18th '01

From: Horatio, Dramaturg

To: Luke, Artistic Director

Re: HAMLET

Shakespeare could have written a Richard II/Bolingbroke, Hal/Harry Hotspur double in Hamlet/Fortinbras. But he has chosen to make the double between one man and his conscience:

"Thus conscience does make cowards of us all." (IIIi)

In the context of a Protestant awareness of moral distinctions, this will be perceived as a cynicism. So it's dazzling that Shakespeare gets round this by, yet again, reinventing that perfect dramatic expression of introspective moral dilemma: the soliloquy.

Horatio

∞∞

```
October 20th '01

Dear Mr Shakespeare,

HAMLET

Do you know that you use the word "brain" or
"brains" eleven times in Hamlet, more than in
any of your other plays?

Loren
```

∞∞

October 21st '01

Dear William,

HAMLET

Here are my top ten quotations:

"This bodes some **strange eruption** to our state" (Ii)

"He waxes **desperate with imagination**" (Iv)

"He raised a sigh so piteous and profound
As it did seem to **shatter all his bulk**
And **end his being**" (IIi)

"So, as a painted tyrant, Pyrrhus stood
And like a neutral to his will and matter
Did nothing" (IIii)

"**Let be**" (Vii)

"A **rhapsody of words**" (IIIiv)

"   What would he do
Had he the motive and the **cue for passion**
That I have?" (IIii)

"What should such fellows as I do **crawling between
earth and heaven?**" (IIIi)

"You would pluck out **the heart of my mystery**" (IIIiii)

"Like sweet bells jangled…
Blasted with ecstasy" (IIIi)

Sasha Radish

Producer

◇◇

October 27th '01

Dear William,

HAMLET

How serious are you that Hamlet should be "fat" ("and scant of breath") (Vii)?

Also: is Ophelia pregnant? She sings:

"'Before you *tumbled* me
You promised me to wed.'" (IVv)

Or does this just imply sex before marriage? It might explain Hamlet's pornographic obsession with Ophelia ("Get thee to a nunnery" (IIIi); "Do you think I mean cunt-ry matters?" (IIIii).) If so, her brother, Laertes, is out of the loop when he warns her that she must not

"   Your chaste treasure open
To his unmastered importunity.
Fear it Ophelia, fear it my dear sister." (Iiii)

When she hands out herbs and flowers "for remembrance", it is a literal act of deflowering, after all.

Yours,

Luke

P.S. Did someone mention that maybe Laertes is gay and is so obsessed with Hamlet himself that he takes it all out on Ophelia? And so Polonius packs him off to Paris to save him from causing more embarrassment.

◇◇

October 28th '01

Dear Mr Shakespeare,

HAMLET

Are there really only two characters in *Hamlet* who achieve their life-goals? They are the two characters who book-end the play. They are the only ones whose names begin with 'F': Francisco and Fortinbras.

Francisco, on watch at the edgy, paranoid opening of the play, is "sick at heart" (Ii). He is desperate to leave and get out of the world of the play – which he does, after a few false exits, never to be seen again.

Fortinbras, who has been conspicuous by his absence virtually throughout the play, turns up at the end to have the last word.

Everyone else is tainted by participating in the story, guilty by association.

Best wishes,

Loren Spiegelei

Literary Department

October 30th '01

Dear William,

HAMLET

Hamlet alludes to Elizabeth's preferred instrument of torture, the dis-jointing wrack:

"The time is out of joint" (Iv).

Elizabeth's Polonius-like spy-master, Robert Cecil, has just installed a new one in the Tower. As so often, your imagery is chillingly concrete. As so often, you are obsessed with the torture-rack – because of how many times it has been inflicted on your fellow writers, I imagine.

Horatio

◇◇

MEMO

October 30th '01

From: Horatio, Dramaturg

To: Luke, Artistic Director

Luke –

"See how occasion laughs me in the face" – *Edward III*, Ii

"How all occasions do inform against me" – *Hamlet*, IViv

Informing being a kind of anonymous, behind-the-back espionage and betrayal. Laughing in your face being an outright mocking of one's authority.

Which is why *Hamlet* is a much better play, more subtle.

Horatio

November 20th '01

Dear Will,

TWELFTH NIGHT, OR WHAT YOU WILL

John Marston has already premièred his play *What You Will* this year – coincidence? *zeitgeist?* or who nicked what from whom?

Is your *What You Will* a passive whatever; or a proactive what you will into being?

And 'Twelfth Night'? It's not really set on the last day of the Christmas festivities, is it? Although it is significant that Twelfth Night is the last chance we get to let our hair down before returning to the hard graft of winter toil.

Have you also called it *Twelfth Night* in homage to January 6th at the beginning of this year when you were performing with The Chamberlain's Men for Elizabeth at Middle Temple, where she was entertaining Don Virginio Orsino? It's surely where you got the lovely name.

In many ways, your play is a throwback to your previous comedies, after the experiment and innovation of *Hamlet*. But, as ever with you, it's a reinvention of your past work, not a slavish reproduction of it. And in its fairytale form – in its sea-storm, twins, deception and disguise, in the social layers of its characterisation, in its prose, verse and lyric poetry – it is close to perfect. So perfect, I wonder if you'll ever write a pure comedy again? It's hard to see how you'll ever top *Twelfth Night* in the comedy stakes.

With very best wishes,

Sasha Radish

Producer

MEMO

November 21st '01

From: Horatio J. Dowden-Adams, Dramaturg

To: Luke Strong, Artistic Director

Re: TWELFTH NIGHT

Shakespeare's new 'comedy' opens with a sad man, surrounded by gloomy-looking courtiers, indulging in what appears to be the posturing melancholy of unrequited love! And he has the prospect of enduring seven more years of this! Although anyone who saw *Love's Labour's Lost*, with its opening gambit declaring three years' abstinence from women, will be alert to the vulnerability of such time restrictions. In fact, he's alerting us to all the themes of the forthcoming play.

The second scene is more cheery – which is odd, because it shows us a chirpy girl who has been shipwrecked, assuming her brother to have been drowned at sea, choosing to disguise herself as a boy – not even a boy, but a de-sexed "eunuch" (Iii). Weird.

The third scene does have some broader comedy, with the gross Sir Toby Belch and his emaciated whipping-boy Sir Andrew Aguecheek – but within the context of a household mourning the loss of a father and son. At least Olivia – who is now in charge as "the honourable lady of the house" (Iv) – doesn't mope as much as Orsino.

So the 'comedy' is like death warmed up – and I mean that as a positive! I think that's why this play is so affecting: our desires and our fears loom either side of the same precipice; our lives are balancing acts where we constantly handicap ourselves with giddiness and queasiness.

Horatio

November 22nd '01

Dear William,

TWELFTH NIGHT

When you wrote *The Comedy of Errors*, when Judith and Hamnet were nine years old, you doubled the number of twins and thus the comic permutations and potential for misunderstandings. Now that Judith is sixteen, and her twin is sadly no longer with us, is that why there's more of a sense of economy in *Twelfth Night*, with just Viola and her twin brother Sebastian?

Best,

Luke

◇◇

MEMO

November 25th '01

From: Horatio J. Dowden-Adams

To: Luke Strong

Re: Twelfth Night

Luke – Most of the confusion is created from dressing up Viola as the boy Cesario (a divisive half-and-half). S/he's like Julia in *The Two Gentlemen of Verona*, or Rosalind in *As You Like It* – less like the cross-dressing women in *The Merchant of Venice*, although the use of a ring (!) is borrowed from that play.

Although Viola seems to be in control, the effect she has on Olivia is dangerous. Olivia's sexual confusion goes into erotic freefall, expressed in her adrenalin-fuelled language:

> "Thy tongue, thy face, thy limbs, actions and spirit
> Do give thee fivefold blazon – not so fast –
> Soft, soft! –
> Unless the master were the man – How now!

Even so quickly may one catch the plague?
Methinks I feel this youth's perfections
With an invisible and subtle stealth
To creep in at mine eyes. Well, let it be – " (Iv)

Everything moves along because the characters act impetuously:

"Who'er I woo, myself would be his wife!" (Iiv),

says Viola, who has fallen immediately for Orsino. Why? We shouldn't stop to ask. Because if we did, we'd wonder why such a spunky girl would fancy such a morbid tragedy queen! The speed is important, because we shouldn't question either why Viola felt it necessary to go to Orsino's court *in disguise* in the first place, but just accept that it's crucial to the dramatic impediment:

"Disguise I see thou art wickedness" (IIii),

she appreciates when Olivia is "charmed" by her Cesario "outside" (IIii). No concrete reason for her disguise is offered, though she does justify it to the Sea Captain, spuriously:

"   I can sing
And speak to him in many sorts of music" (Iii).

But when does she ever? Did Shakespeare drop the idea; or just didn't give it a second thought?

He has composed some of the most exquisite lyrics for Feste, in a play which celebrates music immortally in its opening line:

"If music be the food of love, play on!" (Ii)

I enjoy the theatricality too, supremely embodied in Viola's role-playing, as she's only too aware when trying to play Cesario playing Orsino's messenger before a line of veiled women:

VIOLA   'Most radiant, exquisite, and unmatchable
               beauty' – I pray you tell me if this be the lady

of the house, for I never saw her. I would be loath to cast away my speech: for besides that it is excellently well penned, I have taken great pains to con it…

OLIVIA   Whence come you, sir?

VIOLA   I can say little more than I have studied and the question's out of my part. Good gentle one, give me modest assurance if you be the lady of the house, that I may proceed in my speech.

OLIVIA   Are you a comedian?

VIOLA   No, my profound heart; and yet, by the very fangs of malice, I swear I am not that I play… [etc.] (Iv)

Such exquisite prose. And Viola is so in her part that, like Olivia, we can not help but fall in love with her/him.

Fabian is less subtle in his theatrical conceit when he witnesses the cross-gartered, yellow-stockinged Malvolio:

"If this were played upon a stage now, I could condemn it as an improbable fiction." (IIIiv)

Clumsy it may sound, and yet it's a masterstroke. We don't condemn it. We feel it to be rooted in reality. And, at the same time, we admire the author's concoction.

Author! Author!

Horatio

December 2nd '01

Dear William,

TWELFTH NIGHT: ACTORS

It seems to me that Olivia's steward Malvolio should be played by the same actor who has just played Polonius (and who played Julius Caesar not long before that).

> "I was killed i' the'Capitol. Brutus killed me." (*Hamlet* IIIii)

The role is in similar territory, and there are echoes in the language:

> "Now is the woodcock near the gin" (IIv),

observes Fabian excitedly from the box tree as Malvolio is about to discover the planted letter he'll assume to be Olivia's;

> "Ay, springes to catch woodcocks" (*Hamlet*, Iiii),

spits Polonius to his daughter Ophelia of Hamlet's declaration of love to her.

With Malvolio, like Polonius, you give us a surprisingly sympathetic portrait of vanity "notoriously abused" (IVii+Vi). We're not allowed to warm to him at first:

> "O, you are sick of self-love, Malvolio" (Iv),

Olivia scorns him. But because of the persistent cruelty he receives from the wilful hands of Belch, Maria, Fabian, Feste and (witlessly) Aguecheek, you make us feel sorry for him. His eventual madness is humiliating, incarcerated like a lunatic-thief, with Feste role-playing the chopped-logic confessor Sir Topaz (IVii). This scene is uncomfortable in many ways, not least because it holds up the rest of the plot – we haven't seen Orsino for a good while (not since IIiv); and Viola is out of the picture. I'm tempted to ask you if it can be trimmed in performance, or placed earlier? It's a fine line you're treading throughout the play between main plot and subplot. (In *Much Ado About Nothing* the Benedick-Beatrice subplot took over from the Hero-Claudio main plot. In *Twelfth Night*, the Malvolio sub-plot threatens to do the same. However, as a whole, *Twelfth Night* is a more balanced play.)

I like the fact you showcase your acting ensemble, creating eleven equal roles which play to each of the performer's strengths.

Well fairly equal. Fabian is the dullest. Who gets to play him? Actually, why have him in the play at all? Maria can do everything he does, and I can't see that it's a doubling issue. Antonio is a bit of a thankless part too; although he could be played gay – like his namesake in *The Merchant of Venice* – and he does gain in character as the play progresses:

"Notable pirate, thou salt-water thief." (V)

I'd like to see him, rather than Fabian, double with the Sea Captain so that the same actor rescues both siblings from the storm.

Sir Toby Belch is a short-straw role too. Yet it is the longest part in the play with 13% of the dialogue: 152 speeches in ten scenes to Viola's 121 in eight. That's a lot of lines for an older actor to learn, don't you think? And yet he's upstaged by all around him. Even his eventual marriage to Maria takes place off-stage and is hastily reported (Vi). I suppose you do this because his is the practical/realistic/cynical portrait of what love might eventually amount to, and you don't want to spoil the younger generation's party as they pair up with their idealistic aspirations for the future.

It's probably the "dormouse valour" (IIIii) of Sir Andrew Aguecheek (6% of the dialogue, 88 speeches in eight scenes) that we'll warm to most. I like the way he's set-up by Sir Toby as a highly accomplished intellectual of creative talent –

"He plays o'the'viol-de-gamboys and speaks three or four languages, word for word without book, and hath all the good gifts of nature" (Iiii) –

only to undermine this impression himself when he first appears and doesn't even recognise the French word "pourquoi?" (Iiii). And then there is the sadness with which Sir Andrew Aguecheek delivers:

"I was adored once too." (IIiii)

It has a pathos that will break all our hearts.

With much love,

Bob Castle

Director

December 8th '01.

Dear William,

Although you name Viola only once – at the end in Act V – her name, Olivia's and Malvolio's are all derivations and corruptions of each other – appropriately within a story which folds in on itself, self-referentially. But what about *Mal*volio/*Ben*volio from *Romeo & Juliet* – bad/good? Are they related?

Yours,

Horatio

◇◇◇

December 10th '01

Dear William,

FOOLS

On reflection, I wonder if your wise fools are as successful as they could be. Maybe I was too harsh on Will Kemp, dismissing his natural fools? Should we reconsider Launce and Costard and Bottom and Gobbo and Dogberry versus Touchstone and your clown-fool Feste? Bottom's childlike incorrigibility is surely more sublime than Touchstone or Feste's prickly, adult wit?

Armin will appreciate Feste's

"Better a witty fool than a foolish wit" (Iv);

and:

"They that dally nicely with words may quickly make them wanton"   (Viola, IIIi);

and:

"I am indeed not her fool but her corrupter of words."
(IIIi)

131

But so much of what Feste says is clever-clever and will irritate. Viola summarises his character:

> "This fellow is wise enough to play the Fool,
> And to do that well craves a kind of wit.
> He must observe their mood on whom he jests,
> The quality of persons, and the time,
>   … This is a practice
> As full of labour as a wise man s art…" (IIIi)

This is clearly what you're trying to achieve with these new fools, but in reality I fear they fall short of the mark.

Yours,
Sasha Radish
Producer

◇◇

December 12th '01

Dear Mr Shakespeare,

Like "Viola" (V), "Feste" is only named once (IIiv) and is most frequently called "fool" by the other characters. His speeches are indicated as "Clown" in your script. Are you unable to name him because you're not sure who he is?

Yours,

Loren

Lit. Dept.

December 15th '01

Dear William,

TROILUS & CRESSIDA

Now this is a turn up for the books – or should I say *from* the books? I detect Chapman's Homer, Chaucer's *Troilus & Criseyde* and Robert Henryson's *The Testament of Cresseid* in your new play *Troilus & Cressida*. And, of course, all those plays by Euripides.

It's been bubbling away in your mind for a while, I think, and you mentioned it in passing in your most recent play, *Twelfth Night*, with the Clown Feste fishing for another coin from Cesario/Viola:

"I would play Lord Pandarus of Phrygia, sir, to bring a Cressida to this Troilus." (IIIi)

Twelfth Night was a bitter-sweet comedy. *Troilus & Cressida* is just very sour:

"O world, world, world!" (Vx),

moans Pandarus at the end of the play. Are you all right? Not that writing an anti-heroic play about squabbling Greek and Trojan heroes is necessarily an indication of your descent into an embittered manic depression, but I have to ask.

I'm not asking for an ordered Elizabethan World Picture, but there's something in Ulysses' speech, for instance, that makes me feel all isn't as it seems, and it makes me wonder about you:

"   O when degree is shaked...
The enterprise is sick. How should communities,
Degrees in schools and brotherhoods in cities,
Peaceful commerce from dividable shores,
The primogenitive and due of birth,
Prerogative of age, crowns, sceptres, laurels,
But by degree stand in authentic place?
Take but degree away, untune that string,
And hark what discord follows!" (Iiii)

(You know this will be taken out of context by conservatives and reactionaries, who will ignore the fact Ulysses delivers it with slippery expediency and cunning, all for political gain, cynically manipulating Agamemnon, don't you?)

It is effective "beginning in the middle" (Prologue), when the stalemate siege of Troy has already been dragging on for seven years. But picking the scab on the wound of the Trojan War to release the festering pus beneath... And I'm not just talking about Achilles' malcontent clown, the "crusty botch of nature" (Vi) Thersites; or the leering exploits of Uncle Pandarus pimping Cressida for Troilus; or Achilles indulging "his masculine whore" (Vi) Patroclus. All heroic values are corrupted, let alone moral values. All these mythical creatures are cut down to flawed, pygmy-human size.

The women – to whom Euripides gives the floor, spot-lit, centre-stage – get short shrift in your play. Up until the final act, where Andromache gets to say her piece and Cassandra does more babbling prophesies of doom (Viii – you can cut her from IIiii), I did wonder whether you'd deliberately left out all the women to isolate Cressida, whored in a soldier's world?

I'm discounting the scene (IIIi), with fazed-dazed Helen simpering on Paris' arm. In my view, she shouldn't appear in the play at all. Because she's omnipresent.

Yours,

Luke Strong

Artistic Director

December 20th '01

Dear William,

TROILUS & CRESSIDA

The disturbing thing about the moral corruption in your play is that it impregnates everybody's language. So we get Cressida riffing with Pandarus on the grotesque image of Troilus' unshaven youth:

PANDARUS   You know he has not past three or four hairs on his chin…

CRESSIDA   … Alas, poor chin, many a wart is richer. (Iii)

We get her knowing sexuality:

"They swear all lovers swear more performance than they are able, and yet reserve an ability that they never perform."
(IIIii)

Pandarus' VD-ridden despair about pimping at the end of the play is a queasy, nasty echo of this:

"Why should our endeavour be so desired and the performance so loathed?" (Vx)

You're attracted to doomed lovers. Troilus & Cressida are like Romeo & Juliet, similarly "waked by the lark" (*Troilus & Cressida*, IVii; "It was the lark" *Romeo & Juliet*, IIIv) after their only night of making love together. But it's the exploitation of Cressida as a commodity, and Troilus' jealousy, which dooms them. So the insistence of the Greeks on each taking a turn to kiss their new hostage, Cressida, is more like a ritualised gang rape in your *mise-en-scène* than the mere paying of due respect:

NESTOR   Our general doth salute you with a kiss…

ULYSSES   'Twere better she were kissed in general. (IVv)

It's uncomfortable stuff.

Yours,

Luke Strong

Artistic Director

◇◇

December 31st '01

Dear Mr Shakespeare,

Is it a coincidence that Troilus is also the name of Petruchio's spaniel in *The Taming of the Shrew*? (*Shrew*, IVi)

Yours,

Loren

Literary Department

◇◇

March 17th '02

Dear William,

Why are you so obsessed with the alleged aphrodisiac properties of Sir Walter Raleigh's humble potato?! You got Falstaff all excited by them in the climax to The Merry Wives of Windsor:

> **"Let the sky rain potatoes, let it thunder to the tune of 'Greensleeves'!"   (Vv)**

And here you are again with Thersites' lewd coupling of Troilus and Cressida:

> **"How the devil luxury, with his fat rump and potato-finger, tickles these together! Fry, lechery, fry!" (Vii)**

Chips in the canteen will never seem the same again!

Yours,

Lionel Farthing

Executive Producer

◇◇

May 26th '03

Dear William,

The death of Elizabeth could be the making of the Lord
Chamberlain's men. Once this Plague is over – if ever there
was a judgement on the death of one monarch and the
investiture of the next, then this Plague is surely it – I believe
that James will adopt your company as his own: The King's
Men. It will give you security. But it will inevitably bring you
additional obligations.

Best wishes,

Manfred Mild

Editorial Director

◇◇

December 12th '03

Dear Will,

Would you mind commiserating with Ben Jonson over the
loss of his 7 year old son in this recent bout of the Plague?
You'll know how he feels.

Thanks.

Dickie B.

December 31ˢᵗ '03

Dear William,

SEJANUS

What a controversy! Jonson's going to be summoned to appear before the Privy Council to answer charges of "Popery and Treason". And it was The King's Men's production of his new play **Sejanus** which was the catalyst for this latest charge against him.

I know you performed in it. Jonson's now implying that you helped him out with the rewrites too. Did you?

Lionel Farthing

Executive Producer

◇◇

MEMO

January 2ⁿᵈ '04

To: Luke Strong, Artistic Director

From: Horatio J. Dowden-Adams, Dramaturg

Re: THE TRAGEDY OF OTHELLO, THE MOOR OF VENICE

The subtitle to *The Tragedy of Othello* has echoes of the Venetian intolerance and prejudice in *The Merchant of Venice*. *The Moor of Venice* sizzles, rubbing dark exoticism up against golden Renaissance sophistication. And yet Venice is just the backdrop to a Prologue, in effect. The majority of the play is set on the isle of Cyprus, that outpost of the Western Christian world on the frontier of the Eastern, Ottoman Empire of the infidel.

Shakespeare surprises us further by making the Moor a Christian convert General who leads the military campaign against the Muslim Turk. He is no devilish infidel, unlike

Aaron in *Titus Andronicus*. In fact, it is the white Iago who is a "demi-devil" (Vii). His soliloquy, rounding off the Venice scenes, is an evil invocation of black magic:

"I ha't; it is engendered: Hell and night
Must bring this monstrous birth to the world's light." (Iiii)

(How much more complex Iago is than his predecessor, Don John in *Much Ado*.)

When Othello kisses the wife that he has murdered as he takes his own life "to die upon a kiss" (Vii), we will of course feel the echoes of Romeo and Juliet. But that was puppy love compared to this. *Othello* is a painfully mature play.

Horatio

◇◇

19/1/04

Dear William,

OTHELLO

I do worry after *Troilus & Cressida*, and now *Othello*, that something is going on (or not) in your own sex life and/or marriage and you're pouring it all into these plays: "When I love thee not Chaos is come again" (IIIiii). Of course there's been marital discord in your plays before – between Adriana and Antipholus of Ephesus in *The Comedy of Errors*; or Ford's jealousy in *The Merry Wives of Windsor*. But nothing quite like this:

"   Jealous souls will not be answered so;
They are not jealous for the cause,
But jealous for they are jealous: 'tis a monster
Begot upon itself, born of itself." (IIIiv)

This can apply to all jealousies – professional jealousies in the theatre, for instance; as a playwright and performer you know all about that! – but you apply it specifically to sexual jealousy. The harrowing scene in which Iago winds Othello up into a (second) fit-inducing frenzy has Othello expressing violent, vengeful-jealous thoughts about Desdemona:

"I will chop her into messes." (IVi)

It is deeply disturbing.

Iago's wife Emilia has been around the block; she's got desires. But she is realistic about them. And, over a decade on, you seem to have her answering Kate in *The Taming of the Shrew*, as the Widow should have done:

"   I do think it is their husbands' faults
If wives do fall... Let husbands know
Their wives have sense like them. They see and smell
And have their palates for both sweet and sour
As husbands have. What is it that they do
When they change us for others? Is it sport?
I think it is. And doth affection breed it?
I think it does. Is't frailty that thus errs?
It is so too. And have not we affections?
Desires for sport? And frailty, as men have?
Then let them use us well; else let them know
The ills we do, their ills instruct us so." (IViii)

We respect Emilia. And my faith in your admiration for wives in general, and your wife in particular, is restored.

Best wishes,

Luke Strong

Artistic Director

<><><><><><><><><><><><><><><><><><><><><><><><><><><><><><><><><><><><>

February 2nd '04

Dear William,

And I'm worried about your drinking. In *Henry IV*, for example, it was fun. Now it's maudlin. In Iago's and Cassio's take on booze, and even Othello's views on partying, I'm hearing a *cri de coeur* from an author in fear of his level of alcohol intake.

It's the curse of our profession, I know. We're crap at winding down soberly after a performance, what with all the anticipation of performing compounded by the adrenalin high of being up on stage in front of an audience. Othello's advice about leaving a party when it's still fun, rather than being chucked out with the waste, is sound but too often unheeded by our ilk:

> "Let's teach ourselves the honourable stop
> Not to outsport discretion." (IIiii)

So I worry about you in the light of the Iago and Cassio binge-drinking scene. It starts off being a Mediterranean, Italian man's view of the league table of Northern European drinking lads:

> "Your Dane, your German, and your swag-bellied Hollander
> – drink, ho! – are nothing to your English… Why he drinks
> you with facility your Dane dead drunk; he sweats not to
> overthrow your Alemain; he gives your Hollander a vomit ere
> the next pottle can be filled." (IIiii)

Iago then gets the tea-total (recovering-alcoholic-in-denial?) Cassio mindlessly drunk. Cassio bitterly regrets his loss of "reputation" (IIiii):

> "Drunk? And speak parrot? And squabble? Swagger?
> Swear? And discourse fustian with one's own shadow?
> O, thou invisible spirit of wine, if thou hast no name to be
> known by, let us call thee devil!… O God, that men shall put
> an enemy in their mouths to steal away their brains." (IIiii)

Is there anything I can do to help? Is the booze affecting your output? Is it getting you down?

Much love,

Luke Strong

February 18th '04

Dear Mr Shakespeare,

OTHELLO

I just wanted to write you a fan letter to say
I just so love how you work a prop: Othello
jealously hankers after the hanky which he
believes proves Desdemona and Cassio's hanky-
panky!

Neat!

But can I ask why do you plant something so
crucial to the outcome of the plot so late in
the play (IIIiii)?

Yours,

Loren Spiegelei

Literary Assistant

◇◇◇

March 15th '04

Dear William,

Have you ever thought of writing a writer's manual, a how-to guide
to playwriting? If ever you do, then I think you've hit upon your
title! It's when Cassio protests that he's unable to sing the praises of
Desdemona high enough – while at the same time revealing your own
ability to do so:

> "   He hath achieved a maid
> That paragons description and wild fame,
> One that excels the quirks of blazoning pens
> And in the essential vesture of creation
> Does bear all excellency." (IIi)

Actually, two titles:

> The Quirks of Blazoning Pens;

or:

Best,

Harriet Cumpton-Hawksley

Senior Executive Publishing VP

P.S. I don't know about the soap opera of domestic tragedy, but the passions of *Othello* will certainly make grand opera.

◇◇

April 9th '04

Dear William,

MEASURE FOR MEASURE

Your new play *Measure for Measure* is a public, political play, daring in these politically sensitive times (although which times *aren't* politically sensitive?) And yet this is expressed through private soul-searching:

"Of government the properties to unfold…" (Ii)

That sets the tone from the off. You invite us to weigh up two extremes:

1) the Duke's licentious society

2) the uptight repression imposed by his brother Angelo (though he's no angel).

Do you remember, by the way, the unfortunately named Sir John *Popham*, Lord Chief Justice, who, in 1597, "hath played *rex* of late among whores and bawds, and persecutes poor pretty wenches out of all pity and mercy"? Did he partially inspire Angelo, representative of the moral hypocrisy of all those types? Or is Angelo and the Duke a veiled, two-fold attack simultaneously on James' moral behaviour and his absenteeism?

You also contrast the masses, the unruly misruled, and the fanatical ruler. Your scene in the courtroom (IIi), between the lewd, impertinent anarchist Pompey Bum and the grey-beard upholder of the Establishment, Escalus, is spot on. Neither side of the social divide can comprehend the language or values of the other. (Escalus: that authoritative moniker, like the Prince in *Romeo & Juliet*; and there's also a hint of the climber in that *escalier* name.)

Measure for Measure portrays a society that has its own authority undermined by the very people on behalf of whom it claims to rule: the more it imposes rules, the more they are broken. And this is because the society is a hypocritical one. You'll ruffle feathers.

Best wishes,

Luke Strong

Artistic Director

◇◇◇

May 12th '04

Dear William,

MEASURE FOR MEASURE

What are the choices when considering how to play Isabella? For every decision that can be taken about her character, the contrary one is equally valid.

On the one hand she is morally virtuous; on the other, she is so stubborn. If she's both, then she may be immature in her vacillation, but mature in her suppressed sexuality. Any choices taken in how to play her would depend on her being tainted by her society – or, on the other hand, *un*tainted by it. And what is that society? 'Vienna.' Really? When? 'Now'. The context of the world of the play, and of the production, and the worlds in which we live outside the playhouse, will influence the decisions of the actor.

It's a great part full of the inconsistencies and contradictions that we all suffer, and to which the self-consciously virtuous are especially prone.

So do you really believe that an adolescent boy can do the role justice?

With very best wishes,

Luke Strong

Artistic Director

◇◇

May 14th '04

Dear William,

I've just received an invitation to *The London Prodigal* First Night. It's claiming to be a play by you, inspired by John Lyly. It's got to be a hoax, hasn't it? Or maybe you did have a say in its development? Though I can't imagine why, after *Measure* and the sewer-world of the Duke and Pompey Bum and Mistress Overdone, you'd want to write a city comedy? But then you've always been full of surprises.

Best wishes,

Bob Castle

Director

◇◇

May 20th '04

Dear William,

Now this has got to be a hoax! The Puritan, or The Widow of Watling Street – surely not by you?!! I wonder if cheeky Thomas Middleton is behind it?

On the subject of whom, we're going to ask Middleton to do a polish of Measure. Hope you're all right with that.

Dekker and Marston and the gang are making the running with these hot-house, city sex comedies, and your **Measure for Measure** could do with a bit more comic relief, if I'm honest.

Incidentally, I think Middleton was a bit peeved that you used the duke-in-disguise-as-a-monk trick that he had in his recent play **The Phoenix**. Although someone should point out to both of you that Marston's just done something similar in **The Malcontent**.

Anyhow, Middleton's a bit of a ubiquitous star at the moment, so we'd do well to get him on board.

Yours,

Lionel Farthing

Executive Producer & Chief Executive

◇◇

June 16th '05

Dear William,

ALL'S WELL THAT ENDS WELL

No it doesn't. And it doesn't begin well or middle well either. It was quite a struggle to stay to the end of the performance.

None of this has any bearing on how much I admired your performance as the volatile King of France:

"Unless thou tell'st me where thou hadst this ring
Thou diest within this hour." (V.iii)

Authoritarian and quite potty!

Love,

Lionelx

146

June 17th '04

Dear William,

ALL'S WELL THAT ENDS WELL

Your play gets off to an odd start, doesn't it? At the Rossillions, in the South of France, they're mourning the Count, six months dead, while lamenting that his son, Bertram, has to attend the King in Paris. All fairly glum. Then Helena, like her namesake in *A Midsummer Night's Dream*, declares her unrequited love for the departed Count and gets into an extended metaphorical and pretty tasteless meditation on virginity with the verbose Parolles (= 'words' in French):

> "Virginity is peevish, proud, idle, made of self-love… Off with't while 'tis vendible… Your old virginity is like one of our French withered pears: it looks ill, it eats drily; marry, 'tis a withered pear; it was formerly better; marry yet 'tis a withered pear." (Iii)

From there on in, you sustain the uneasy tension in this curious, nasty battle of the sexes: sowing your oats v. maintaining your integrity. So when the King of France rewards low-born orphan Helena for curing his sickness (Iiii), by allowing her to choose a husband from all the courtiers present, and she chooses Bertram, Bertram doesn't want her. Which is fair enough, I suppose: he'd rather fight wars and whore his way round Europe. But the King insists, even after Bertram's made his feelings plain:

> "A poor physician's daughter my wife! Disdain
> Rather corrupt me ever!" (IIiii)

Yet she wants to go through with it. Why? And reverse the sexes for a moment: if a woman was being forced into a marriage with a man, we'd be outraged, wouldn't we? Yet you make us feel that she's the wronged party, he the bad guy. Sure, he's Demetrius-like in his contempt for her: "Here comes my clog."

(IIv) But why are these girls such masochists? What do they see in these arrogant youths?

Bertram cannily vows not to consummate the marriage:

"I'll to the Tuscan wars and never bed her." (IIiii)

But when Helena perseveres and, disguised as a pilgrim, pursues him to Florence where she employs the bed-trick, recently used by Isabella in *Measure for Measure*, by having sex with Bertram when he thinks he's deflowering Diana whom he's been pestering –

"Give yourself to my sick desires" (IVii) –

…well… I don't know what to think.

Neither Bertram nor Helena come out of it covered with glory. Helena gets deviously pregnant. And after the most irritating of riddling final scenes – when we know all that's happened but everyone on stage doesn't and so in catching up they get even more tangled in knots – you then deliver a crude, perfunctory *dénouement*.

It's a symptom of something not being quite right with the play as a whole. It's as if you ran out of steam, or confidence, or both – certainly out of love with your characters. Bertram is unrepentant and brags to the last, without a qualm about his treatment of the woman he believes to be Diana:

"   I liked her
And boarded her i'the'wanton way of youth.
She knew her distance and did angle for me,
Madding my eagerness with her restraint." (Viii)

Pairing Helena and Bertram at the end, when only "All yet *seems* well" (Viii) is even more unsatisfactory than having Julia forgive Proteus, whose just attempted to rape his best friend's fiancée, at the end of *The Two Gentlemen of Verona*.

If I was being generous I would offer in your defence your First Lord's metaphor:

148

"The web of our life is of a mingled yarn: good and ill together."

(IViii)

I could argue that the tale you spin is likewise mingled, an uncomfortable tragi-comedy, the strands co-existing uneasily. And that you meant it on purpose.

And I have to confess that you have written an appealing older woman's part in the Countess – to add to the repertory of Tamora in *Titus*, Queen Eleanor in *King John*, Margaret come *Richard III*, and the Duchess of Gloucester/Duchess of York double in *Richard II*.

But I can't help feeling that *All's Well That Ends Well* is as awkward a play as your recent *Troilus & Cressida* and *Measure for Measure*. This troublesome period you've been going through has also thrown up *Othello*. And I know you're about to deliver *Timon of Athens*, which doesn't sound like it's going to be barrel of laughs either. It feels like you're having a wobble.

Whatever. I don't think you'll look back on *All's Well* as your finest hour.

Yours,

Luke Strong

Artistic Director & Joint Chief Executive Elect

P.S. Suggested cuts: Parolles. Enough said. As for Lavatch, the Countess of Rossillion's clown…! Yet again you kill all the laughs with the tediousness of wit. Each time he's on stage it's like drowning in treacle. When Lord Lafew attempts to dismiss Lavatch in exasperation –

"Go thy ways. I begin to be aweary of thee" (IVv) –

we know how he feels.

July 8th '05

Dear William,

ALL'S WELL THAT ENDS WELL

I know we're supposed to avoid the elephant trap of literary biography, but this reluctant young Frenchman Bertram being pressed into marriage: isn't that what was happening in your Silver Street landlords' lives while you were writing this? If so, that might explain why this is one of your least outward-looking plays, with very little more universal matter to be drawn from the fable. Uncharacteristically, you haven't been able to play off your experience against the story you've based it upon.

Yours,

Luke Strong

◇◇

September 2nd '05

Dear William,

What do you think of Samuel Rowley's comical *When You See Me, You Know Me, or the famous Chronicle History of King Henry the Eighth, with the Birth and Virtuous Life of Edward Prince of Wales*? Henry VIII is like your Hal, but in Falstaff's body!

And have you seen the anonymous *Thomas Lord Cromwell* that's been an occasional filler in the repertoire for the past few years, by the way? It is also a Henry VIII play...

Best wishes,

Manfred Mild

Publisher

September 12th '05

Dear Willy,

I can't believe Ben Jonson's in prison again, this time for offending James with his Scots' lampoons in *Eastward Ho!* His co-writer George Chapman, who did that Homer translation, is locked up too. Their other collaborator, John Marston, is protesting his innocence. When will Ben settle down?

Yours,

Ricky Burb.

◇◇

September 14th '05

Dear William,

Thomas Heywood's new play is a bit flash: *If You Know Not Me, You Know Nobody: The Troubles of Queen Elizabeth*. But it's good on her persecution by her Catholic sister, Mary.

Do you think you'll ever write a play explicitly featuring Elizabeth?

Best,

Sasha Radish

Producer

◇◇

September 21st '05

Dear William,

TIMON OF ATHENS

Thomas Middleton has sent me the first draft of your joint effort. I know it's only a fable, but it should come with a government health warning! Talk about cynical: there is no redemption, no reconciliation, no renewal – though Greek war hero Alcibiades does, at the last, spare Athens from the brink of apocalyptic chaos. But only just.

It's a strange experiment, a complete departure from anything you've worked on before – or Middleton for that matter (most unlike *The Honest Whore* two-parter he's just written with Thomas Dekker).

Athenian society, such as it is, is shallow, brittle, dysfunctional. It occupies a world without women (save a couple of whores); a world without families; a world without true friendship (except steward Flavius' unrequited devotion to his master Timon); a world without hope. Money is assumed to be the only means to achieving satisfaction, but it actually feeds an insatiable, self-consuming hunger. I'd say it was a mid-life crisis play – except that Middleton, sixteen years your junior, is in his mid-twenties to your early forties.

It doesn't seem that you can have collaborated that closely, to be honest – that one-off appearance of the Fool near the start (IIii): what's that about?

As it stands, the play's too simplistic, Timon too naïve. His journey from philanthropist to misanthropist lacks dramatic fire. His retreat to the woods outside Athens has the opposite effect of the escape to the melting-pot of love and transformation experienced in the same location by the lovers, mechanicals and fairies in *A Midsummer Night's Dream*.

Maybe you should send it to your former patron and *Venus & Adonis* + *Rape of Lucrece* dedicatee, the Earl of Southampton? It's a kind of tribute to him, in a way, isn't it? Since he came a cropper after borrowing so much against Essex's Rebellion, he's not been able to chuck the cash around in quite the same way amongst us artists, "the world as my confectionary" (IViii). But I'd hate to think of Southampton abandoned by his fickle poets and painters, and, like Timon, being driven into a hermit-like existence outside the city and to suicidal despair:

"The middle of humanity thou never knowest, but the extremity of both ends." (IViii)

"   His wits
Are drowned and lost in his calamities." (IViii).

"I am Misanthropos and hate mankind." (IViii)

Cheer up, William: it might never happen!

Yours,

Luke Strong

Artistic Director & Joint Chief Executive

◇◇

MEMO

September 25th '05

To: Luke, AD+Joint CEO

From: Sasha, Producer

Re: TIMON OF ATHENS

Luke – my hunch is that the play is unlikely to be performed in Shakespeare's lifetime. It will remain in the bottom drawer, a tantalising work-in-progress. Middleton's got other fish to fry – he's just written *A Trick to Catch the Old One*; and he's secretly working on a revenger's tragedy I think. I know Bill's about to deliver his ancient Britain *King Lear* tragic epic (any light relief in that?). Anyway, the anonymous *Timon* which premièred at Inner Temple a couple of years back wasn't that much of a hit, so there's not a lot of commercial sense trying to flog similar goods.

Sasha

October 3rd '05

Dear William,

KING LEAR

I must confess it's come as a bit of a surprise to read your *History of King Lear* so hot on the heels of publication of the Rose's *True Chronicle History of King Leir And His Three Daughters*. Of course, yours is a superior play, but whether it's a Tragedy rather than a History, is open to debate. Yours is a story which, for all concerned, moves from bad to worse. And opening everyone's eyes to the truth of this is what drives the play on ruthlessly and relentlessly towards its endgame.

It is a nihilistic masterpiece – pre-Christian, pagan, primeval. A true Tragedy would recognise an absolute authority. Your characters pathetically try to conjure one, any one, but their experience demonstrates that there is none. You have created a timeless Theatre of the Absurd.

I also suspect that what you have created in the character of Lear is not some ancient old man in his 80s ("Fourscore and upward" he says (IVvii)), but a man in a mid-life crisis. Richard Burbage will create the role and he's still shy of 40. And how old are you? Just into your 40s, at the height of your success, comfortable financially, with early retirement within your grasp. Your daughters, however, are gaining their independence – and may not thank you for all that you've done for them. So you may well lash out:

"How sharper than a serpent's tooth it is
To have a thankless child!" (Iiv)

But you know that is old-fashioned thinking. What do children have to be thankful for if the behaviour of their parent towards them doesn't earn respect? How well we forty-somethings recognise the frustration in Lear's impotent rage:

"I will have such revenges on you both
That all the world shall – I will do such things –

What they are, yet I know not." (IIiv)

Goneril and Regan are new pretenders jostling for power. Part of that process requires them to sever the umbilical cord with their past. As we enter our middle age, we start to forget things; to get more set in our ways; to pretend we haven't heard, when really we're not listening; to fly off the handle over the pettiest of things because we're distracted by something larger that we refuse to share; to grow mad at the maddening world and believe ourselves "More sinned against than sinning" (IIIii). The last thing we can tolerate is a daughter mocking us:

"   O, Sir! You are old.
Nature in you stands on the very verge
Of her confine: you should be ruled and led
By some discretion that discerns your state
Better than you yourself." (IIiv)

How bloody infuriating to fathers self-righteous daughters can be!

Best wishes,

Luke Strong

Artistic Director & Joint Chief Executive & Father of Daughters

◇◇

November 2nd '05

Dear William,

"This great stage of fools" (*Lear*, IVvi)

I take it that although the Fool is called "boy", he is Lear's contemporary? Or older (like *Hamlet*'s Yorick, had he lived). The Fool understands Lear, more than a young court jester ever could. He has the experience, the wisdom and the authority to be critical:

LEAR   Dost thou call me fool, boy?
FOOL   All thy other titles thou hast given away; that
            thou wast born with. (Iiv)

(To which Kent unnecessarily gilds the lily: "This is not altogether Fool, my lord." You should cut that – we're not fools!)

Best,

Bob Castle

Director

◇◇

MEMO

December 1st '05

From: Horatio J. Dowden-Adams, Dramaturg

To: Luke Strong, Artistic Director + Joint CEO

Re: KING LEAR

I think I may have spotted moments of tragic catharsis in the Absurdist, grotesque cruelty.

There is a jet black, grim kind of humour to be had in the parallel story of Gloucester and his two sons. This climaxes with the gruesome eye-gouging of Gloucester:

"   Out, vile jelly!
Where is thy lustre now?" (IIIvii)

The blinded Gloucester is then chucked out of his own home –

"Go thrust him out at gates and let him smell
His way to Dover" (IIIvii) –

just as Gloucester had shut his doors against Lear in the impending storm (IIiv).

Shakespeare has invented a Theatre of Cruelty (he's been heading this way for some time) and I note that he has a question mark over whether to include the coda to Act III where Gloucester's servants express their tender humanity:

"I'll fetch him some flax and white of eggs
To apply to his bleeding face. Now, heaven help him!"

(IIIvii)

Shakespeare's metaphor of blindness – "I stumbled when
I saw," says the blinded Gloucester (IVi) – is limpid. Only
when Lear is stripped of the trappings of kingship and
fatherhood, stripped of clothes and reason can he see himself
and humanity for what it all is: nothing.

"Nothing" reverberates its hollow echo throughout the play:

LEAR	What can you say to draw A third more opulent than your sisters? Speak.
CORDELIA	Nothing, my lord.
LEAR	Nothing?
CORDELIA	Nothing.
LEAR	Nothing will come of nothing. Speak again. (Ii)

"I am better than thou art now: I am a Fool; thou art
nothing." (Iiii)

"Edgar I nothing am." (IIiii)

Each thought system that each character adopts in their
attempt to make order out of the chaos in the world, is
undermined. Edgar articulates a misplaced Stoicism to his
father Gloucester when Gloucester wishes to die:

"   Men must endure
Their going hence even as their coming hither;
Ripeness is all." (Vii)

(To which Gloucester enigmatically responds: "And that's
true too".) This crumb of salvation in a pagan world sounds
like Hamlet, without the defiance:

"We defy augury. There's a special providence in the fall
of a sparrow. If it be now, 'tis not to come. If it be not to

come, it will be now. If it be not now, yet it will come. The readiness is all." (*Hamlet*, Vii)

Edgar's "Ripeness is all" is grimmer.

Edgar's final couplets in the play (I'm sure Shakespeare didn't really mean them to be Albany's as they appear in one of the drafts) are defeatist:

"The weight of this sad time we must obey,
Speak what we feel, not what we ought to say.
The oldest hath borne most. We that are young
Shall never see so much nor live so long." (Viii)

Shakespeare has already given us the language of Doomsday:

KENT   Is this the promised end?

EDGAR   Or the image of that horror?

ALBANY   Fall and cease.   (Viii)

As Kent goes off to die, he is resigned to seeing life as "the rack of this tough world", stretching us all to breaking point (Viii). All mankind is broken in this play. Lear's dying words over the corpse of the daughter he has wronged, is full of negatives:

"   No, no, no life!
Why should a dog, a horse, a rat have life
And thou no breath at all? Thou'lt come no more,
Never, never, never, never, never!..." (Viii)

King Lear is bleak. But therein lies its resounding strength for all eternity.

Horatio

January 5th '06

Dear William,

FOUR PLAYS IN ONE

I'd like you to contribute to the benefit play we've got going with Thomas Middleton and others.

The idea is that we get four writers each to write a one-act play that can be performed all in one evening. They might also help each other out, like in the old days. It's got the working title *Four Plays in One* and Middleton's already well underway with *A Yorkshire Tragedy*. But he's struggling with a domestic quarrelling scene. Can you help?

If you have any thoughts, let me know – bottom-drawer ideas gratefully received! As long as it's not like that idea for a pot-boiler, *The Merry Devil of Edmonton*, you tried to fob me off with! It was wise to pass that on to Thomas Dekker, John Ford and William Rowley.

Many thanks.

Yours,

Luke Strong

Artistic Director & Joint Chief Executive

◇◇

January 30th '06

Dear William,

A YORKSHIRE TRAGEDY

I like what you've helped Middleton pull off. It's as well-structured and as grippingly emotional/emotionally gripping as a miniature Greek tragedy. It's grisly – the more so because it's based on the true story of a melancholic, Yorkshire boor, rejected by snooty London court circles, university academics and financial good fortune. It is a titillating terror-tale. When he batters his wife and murders his kids... Good, gruelling stuff.

Many thanks!

Best wishes,

Luke Strong

Artistic Director & Joint Chief Executive

◇◇

February 2nd '06

Dear William,

It's as if, after *Hamlet* – with all its associations with your dead son and the death of your father – you could only pull off the classically perfect *Twelfth Night* before you hit the buffers. Everything went pear-shaped for you, compounded by the death of Queen Elizabeth. So your regular output of at least a couple of plays a year throughout the '90s dried up, with only sporadic outbursts with the brute *Troilus & Cressida*, the dirty *Measure for Measure*, the brooding *Othello*, the bitter-sweet *All's Well That Ends Well*, the misanthropic *Timon*... It was as if you were no longer comfortable in your creative skin.

Maybe it was the shock of the political controversy that your History Plays heaped upon you, and your concern that you and your fellow dramatists were dicing with death? Maybe it's because you're acting less and less now so aren't so woven into the warp and weft of the theatre? Maybe it's your lack of literal hunger, your father finally making good by you in his will in 1601, when your playwriting was already affording you and your family a comfortable life? Maybe it's because, driven out of London by Plague, you're chilling out in the provinces a bit too often now?

But now, out of the blue, you've excelled yourself with *Macbeth*.

Best wishes,

Manfred Mild
Publisher

February 8th '06

Dear William,

MACBETH

I know how much Christopher Marlowe must haunt you; and, in a sense, *Macbeth* is your *Doctor Faustus*.

Only it's miles better.

All the best,

Sasha Radish

Producer

◇◇◇

February 10th '06

Dear William,

MACBETH

Equivocation is in the ether in Jacobean England and Scotland. It's what Jesuits do, equivocate, since their extreme Catholicism forbids them to lie outright.

"Double, double toil and trouble" (IVi) chant the Witches. Doubleness, as in all your plays crammed with twins and antithesis, has a double-meaning itself: it is both accumulation *and* opposing duality.

Your play is crammed full of doubling and redoubling equivocation. Macbeth vacillates:

"This supernatural soliciting
Cannot be ill, cannot be good…" (Iiii)

Yours,

Horatio

February 11th '06

Dear William,

MACBETH

Macbeth deliberately puts himself into a position of spiritual darkness:

"To know my deed, 'twere best not know myself." (IIii)

He ends in light, forced by Macduff into the open, no longer "cabin'd, cribb'd, confined" (IIIiv) in his bunker, but thrust into the new dawn:

"I 'gin to be aweary of the sun." (Vv)

Life to him is a "candle" which lights

"   fools
The way to dusty death." (Vv)

It's another one of your great tragic roles for our leading actors.

Lady Macbeth began in the light, acting with clarity of purpose, declaring that Duncan will not see out the night:

"   O never
Shall sun that morrow see!" (Iv)

But after they have murdered Duncan, they are unable to tell night from day:

MACBETH   What is the night?

LADY MACBETH   Almost at odds with morning, which is
                                        which? (IIIiv)

Lady Macbeth ends in a harrowing darkness, vulnerable, sleep-walking. She is one of the most extraordinary, mature women you've ever written. Who will play her?

Best wishes,

Bob Castle

Director

MEMO

February 15th '06

From: Horatio, Dramaturg

To: Bob, Director

Re: MACBETH

Bob – Macbeth's servant Seyton (appropriately named) only comes to him on third calling (Viii). The cold-blooded efficiency of Malcolm's new order has his soldiers responding immediately "It shall be done" (Viv).

Macbeth has no loyal allies, forced to hire Kerns, Irish mercenaries, which Macdonwald had done in the battle which opens the play. (Kerns generally get a bad press in Shakespeare's plays:

> "We must supplant those rough rug-headed Kern
> Which live like venom where no venom else
> But only they have privilege to live" (*Richard II*, IIi).)

Ireland, as we know from Essex's disastrous campaign, is an unruly land. It can't be comforting to Malcolm that Ireland is where his brother Donalbain has fled in exile (IIiii). Maybe that's why Malcolm's final, falsely rhyming couplet is ominous?:

> "So thanks to all at once, and to each one,
> Whom we invite to see us crowned at Scone." (Vix)

There have been other signals: Malcolm is greeted thrice: "Hail!" (Vix). So was Macbeth. By the Witches.

Authority may be re-established at the end of the play, but its strength and pedigree are questionable to say the least. The play never recovers from the evil spell cast upon it by its opening scene:

> "When shall we three meet again…" (Ii)

> "What's done is done" (IIIii),

says Lady Macbeth.

"What's done cannot be undone" (Vi),
says Lady Macbeth.
Horatio

◇◇

February 18th '06

Dear William,

THE SCOTTISH PLAY

Were you unnerved making Evil so tangible in this play? We're so superstitious in the theatre that we won't call it *M******* but *The Scottish Play*, stepping outside the dressing-room and turning around three times and such like.

We know King James likes plays about witchcraft – and you've quickly followed the success of Marston's *Sophonisbra* which presented witchcraft just as disturbingly as you do in your play. Plus you get Banquo to spell out his legacy:

"Myself should be the root and father
Of many kings" (IIIi),

Banquo is James' ancestor. So this play is going to go down very well in private performance at Court, as well as in the public playhouse.

Yours,

Luke Strong

Artistic Director & Joint Chief Executive

MEMO

February 28th '06

From: Lionel Farthing, Joint CEO

To: Luke Strong, Joint CEO

Re: MACBETH

Luke –

It's unproduceable! Those witches! That moving wood!

However, we could defer the running costs to the new financial year. You'll appreciate that we've used up all our actor weeks for this year as it is. And what with the Marlowe retrospective in the autumn and the need to get a satisfactory Christmas title as an alternative to the panto, we just can't take big risks on new works. But you'll still have to reduce its scale.

Lionel

◇◇

MEMO

March 1st '06

From: Luke

To: Lionel

Re: MACBETH

Lionel – I'm going to ask Thomas Middleton to do a polish – to give us *more* of the witch stuff, which (pardon the pun) he'll take from his own play *The Witch*. Then we'll have a sure-fire box office hit.

Luke

May 5th '06

William -

How's the drinking? Provoking the desire but taking away the performance? (Porter, *Macbeth*, IIiii)

Richy B.

◇◇

June 7th '06

Dear William,

Another Plague! These enforced theatre closures aren't helping your flow, are they?

I have been thinking of your acting and how it has fed into your writing up to now. You never get to play the lead, just the bit-parts, and the old men and ghosts at that – because you're bald, I guess! (Sorry: balding.) But this gives you a worm's-eye view of your own plays. The Ghost of Hamlet's father in *Hamlet*; Old Adam in *As You Like It* – they both disappear from the action after a while. So, what do you do for the rest of the play? I know you'll double up a small part by taking a cameo turn as Osric in *Hamlet*; or as the late-appearing Jacques II, "second son of old Sir Rowland" (Viv), in *As You Like It* . Meanwhile, do you slip into your audience to observe and listen to them observing and listening to your play?

Why do you still act? Do you need the money? I know that writing plays doesn't earn you that much – between £4 and £6 per comission or thereabouts, and split with the collaborators where appropriate. (A fine for an actor not turning up to a performance is a stiff £1; the purchase of a decent frock for performance is a whopping great £20.) There will be modest performance royalties if the play goes well, but all playwrights have to churn plays out to make a living, even you. You can never be sure which one is going to be a hit and survive in the repertoire.

You sell your plays for the commission fee to the commissioning company – it's the company who sells the play-text to the publisher to make a bit of money for itself, or to prevent other 'Bad Quartos' from stealing potential audience. Because you have an interest in the King's Men company, in addition to your stake in the theatre building of the Globe, you have a share in the "Joint Stock" – the three assets of the company: the costumes, the props and the play scripts. So, curiously, you might be making more money out of publishing your plays as the management than you do as a playwright!

Much love,

Manfred Mild

Publisher

◇◇

June 30th '06

Dear Mr Shakespeare,

Your vocabulary is awesome. So many new words, phrases, flowing from your pen and into the public consciousness. Your capacity for word-hoarding is ten times that of the next man. How do you do it?

Best wishes,

Loren Spiegelei

Literary Assistant

July 12th '06

Dear William,

I've been reading your draft of *Antony & Cleopatra* in which Cleopatra has a premonition that:

> "   The quick comedians
> Extemporally will stage us and present
> Our Alexandrian revels: Antony
> Shall be brought drunken forth and I shall see
> Some squeaking Cleopatra boy my greatness
> I'the posture of a whore." (Vii)

Clever. Alienating. But it could be a very unflattering thing for the squeaking boy actor to have to say before an audience!

Don't you long for a woman to play the female roles? Have they been played by women in private, in the Elizabethan or Jacobean court, to your knowledge?

There are closet women playwrights: Frances Merbury, who wrote *A Marriage Between Wit and Wisdom* just before your time in 1579; Mary Herbert, who wrote her Antony & Cleopatra play *Antonius* in 1590, just as you were toying with others on the History Plays. Do women perform on stage clandestinely? In crowd scenes, perhaps even with occasional lines: "Tear him for his bad verses!" (*Julius Caesar*, IIliii)? Front of House staff, who gather the money in lieu of a ticket (a penny in the yard; a shilling in the poshest seats) have been known to join in the action on stage to swell a scene. And some of the FOH staff are women…

Best wishes,

Sasha Radish

Producer

July 18th '06

Dear William,

We all know bad acting when we see it:

> " Like a strutting player whose conceit
> Lies in his hamstring, and doth think it rich
> To hear the wooden dialogue and sound
> 'Twixt his stretched footing and the scaffoldage…"
> (*Troilus & Cressida*, Iiii)

But what is good acting? Is it as Hamlet outlines to the players? Or is he Ham-ming it up?

> " … Do not saw the air too much with your hand thus, but use all gently; for in the very torrent, tempest, and, as I may say, whirlwind of your passion, you must acquire and beget a temperance that may give it smoothness… Be not too tame neither, but let your own discretion be your tutor. Suit the action to the word, the word to the action, with this special observance, that you o'erstep not the modesty of nature. For anything so o'erdone is from the purpose of playing, whose end both at the first and now, was and is, to hold as 'twere the mirror up to nature… And let those that play your clowns speak no more than is set down for them… " (IIIii)

Apart from your dig against clowns (it can't be Hamlet's: there are no clowns in *The Murder of Gonzalez*, nor his *Mousetrap* rewrites), the rest sounds authentically like an overexcited writer/director/producer gushing around backstage before the first night. Except that Hamlet is a student prince, an amateur telling professionals how it's done:

> "To hold as 'twere the mirror up to nature." (IIIii)

Is this really what you believe about the artifice of great acting?

Acting is a projection of our *true* nature, not a naturalistic, pale reflection. In *A Midsummer Night's Dream*, you have Theseus talk about:

> "The poet's eye, in a fine frenzy rolling,
> Doth glance from heaven to earth, from earth to heaven,
> And as imagination bodies forth
> The forms of things unknown, the poet's pen

Turns them to shapes, and gives to airy nothing
A local habitation and a name.
Such tricks hath strong imagination..." (Vi)

Yours,

Bob Castle

Director

◇◇

December 18th '06

Dear Mr Shakespeare,

THE TRAGEDY OF ANTONY AND CLEOPATRA

Or should that be:

THE TRAGEDY OF ANTONY , AND CLEOPATRA

What's in a comma? You may well ask! But since
you use both versions of the title in your
script, we need to know whether we will have
a leading "pair so famous" (Vii) sharing the
star billing? Or are we just going with our
leading man, (comma) and his co-star?

Thanks.

Yours,

Loren Spiegelei

Literary Assistant

December 19th '06

Dear William,

ANTONY & CLEOPATRA

Egypt and Rome, Woman and Man, Venus and Mars, Sea and Land, Heart and Head, Emotion and Reason, Microcosm and Macrocosm – all so bound up in this play. The entire world is affected by the actions of a few people: the contrary mood-swinging of our protagonists, Antony and Cleopatra, and the steadfastness and fastidiousness of their antagonist, Octavius.

Antony and Cleopatra are love-hate lovers – like extreme versions of Berowne and Rosaline, Beatrice and Benedick, even Kate and Petruchio before them – childish, though in their mature years. They represent the passing of the old "libertine" (Ili) order. Octavius brings with him the new, puritanical age. He is a Machiavellian master, and I keep thinking of the cold calculation of:

"They are the lords and owners of their faces" (Sonnet 94),

in your forthcoming Sonnet sequence. Yet for all that Caesar conquers fortune where Antony is crushed by it, for all the political victory of Caesar and the deaths of Antony and Cleopatra, Caesar is unable to master the narrative. Consummate politician that he is, he does, of course, claim conquest:

"   Their story is
No less in pity than his glory which
Brought them to be lamented." (Vii)

But it's "their story" which your play celebrates, not "his glory".

In fact, it is Antony's loyal, wry factotum, Enobarbus (who earns only a brief mention in your Plutarch source), who appears to be in charge of the narrative. He dies of thinking – there is nothing else to explain it –

"And earns a place i'the story." (IIIxiii)

You've written the part of Enobarbus for yourself, haven't you? So you will get to deliver the glorious speech about Cleopatra:

"The barge she sat in, like a burnished throne
Burned on the water: the poop was beaten gold;
Purple the sails, and so perfumed that
The winds were love-sick with them…" (IIii)

What a beautiful rewrite of North's Plutarch:

"Her barge in the river Cydnus, the poop whereof was gold, the sailes of purple…"

Enobarbus is you, William Shakespeare, playmaker, speaking Chorus-like from the heart of your own play.

Best wishes,

Luke Strong

◇◇◇

December 20th '06

Dear Mr Shakespeare,

I don't suppose you saw *Caesar & Pompey* when it was on at Trinity College, Oxford over a decade ago? And did you ever read Samuel Brandon's closet dramas *Cleopatra* (1593) or *The Virtuous Octavia* (1598)?

Loren Spiegelei

December 21ˢᵗ '06

Dear William,

Do you think Antony & Cleopatra is in danger of going pear-shaped in performance? I think you kill off both Enobarbus and Antony a bit too soon, as you did Mercutio in Romeo & Juliet in my view. After all the urgency, helped by the messengers speeding the plot along and the short, sharp scenes, the fag end of the play runs the risk of limping to its inevitable conclusion (the death of Cleopatra; the triumph of Octavius) as it bleeds to death, haemorrhaging momentum.

Best,

Lionel Farthing

Executive

◇◇

January 3ʳᵈ '07

Dear William,

ANTONY & CLEOPATRA

I like the fact that Antony's servants have significant names, like Macbeth's Seyton. I'm thinking of Eros (the god of love) and Scarrus, literally battle-scarred, displaying his prowess as soldier and unflinching commitment in battle. To him you give the despairing dispatch from the front line:

"   We have kissed away
Kingdoms and provinces...
The noble ruin of her magic, Antony,
Claps off his sea-wing and, like a doting mallard,
Leaving the fight in height, flies after her.
I never saw an action of such shame;
Experience, manhood, honour, ne'er before
Did violate so itself." (IIIx)

Also, do I detect a touch of Elizabeth and her ladies-in-waiting in Cleopatra's volatile behaviour towards, and knowing sexual banter with, her serving women, Charmian and Iras?

Yours,

Horatio J. Dowden-Adams

Dramaturg

◇◇

January 5th '07

Dear William,

ANTONY & CLEOPATRA

Is Taurus, Octavius' loyal lieutenant, the smallest named part in any of your plays? "My lord?" is all he says (IIIviii) – yet you carefully set him up in the previous scene so that we're all expecting him; and he's crucial to Octavius' Battle of Actium strategy, to hold back with his ground force until his navy has vanquished Antony's at sea:

"   Our fortune lies
Upon this jump." (IIIviii)

And to give him extra clout, you give him a butch name: Taurus: The Bull.

Best wishes,

Horatio J. Dowden-Adams

Dramaturg and Trainee Producer

February 28th '08

Dear William,

Congratulations on the birth of your grand-daughter,
Elizabeth! Quite a brood of women you now have up
in Stratford. You must be proud – though feeling older,
Grandad!

Best wishes,

Richard B.

◇◇

MEMO

April 9th '08

From: Horatio, Dramaturg and Trainee Producer

To: Luke, Artistic Director

Re: CORIOLANUS

This is an extraordinarily politicised, proudly personal
play with Coriolanus, all patrician swagger and absolutist
charisma, contemptuously pouting and spitting his plosives:
"*P*eo-*P*le!"

The war-mongering patricians vie with conspiratorial civil
servant tribunes, both parties exploiting the malleability of
The Peo-Ple: citizens who are impotent to map out their own
historical destinies; and fickle, as they are in *Julius Caesar*,
or in Jack Cade's uprising in *Henry VI Part 2*, or in the City
rebellion quelled in Shakespeare's contribution to *Sir Thomas
More*.

Coriolanus may be not be as mainstream as either *Julius Caesar*
or that play's long-time-in-coming sequel *Antony & Cleopatra*,
but Shakespeare has created a mighty, arrogant central
character.

He's a Man's Man. And yet he's ruled by his Mum. Like Queen Eleanor to King John, or Queen Margaret to her brood in *Henry VI*, Volumnia is a tough matriarch:

> "Had I a dozen sons... I had rather had eleven die nobly for their country, than one voluptuously surfeit out of action." (Iiii)

With no father figure in the play, Volumnia wears the trousers. The Romans – like the Brits – frequently like to imagine that they are descended from mythical Troy; by association, Volumnia claims the "bragged progeny" (Iviii) for herself and her son:

> "   The breasts of Hecuba
> When she did suckle Hector, looked not lovelier
> Than Hector's forehead when it spit forth blood
> At Grecian sword contemning." (Iiii)

Her maternal instincts are martial. When Coriolanus' sensitive wife, Virgilia, on hearing of his wounds in battle wails

> "Oh no, no, no" (IIi),

his Mother responds with casual steeliness:

> "Oh, he is wounded: I thank the gods for it." (IIi)

Though a mighty warrior, Coriolanus is accused by the citizens at the beginning of the play of feeble motives in fighting for Rome:

> "Though soft-conscienced men can be content to say it was for his country, he did it to please his mother." (Ii)

Aufidius at the end of the play mocks him with the ultimate insult:

> "Thou boy of tears!" (Vvi)

Coriolanus' tragic flaw is that he's a Mummy's Boy. Discuss!
Horatio

July 6th '08

Dear Mr Shakespeare,

CORIOLANUS

Are you a unique, creative genius working in the isolated playground of your scintillating intellect and poetic imagination? Or are you merely the product of your historical circumstances, guided by events and the mechanics of your age? I ask because there's a critical debate raging which uses *Coriolanus* as its battleground.

The argument is centred on what seems to be a spark for the play: the corn riots (as reported by Plutarch) which incite the rebellion of the people at the start of your play – and also echoing the English corn riots last year.

Personally, I don't mind what drives you. I suspect, as with most writers, it's a bit of everything: your genius letting you down on off days; your times not always being so inspiring that you can't abstract yourself from them. I like the fact that you apply yourself to the source material *and* to your contemporary news, not because you're writing an historical chronicle or a docu-drama, but because you're exploring the political and the personal, the contrast between people and patricians, the have-nots and the haves. The corn riots which open the play are both a catalyst and the symptom of the dramatic tension in the nation and in your play. You understand the basic human need for food, the hunger that drives starving men to desperate measures. But you also appreciate what drives the contempt of a hero whose words to the rabble are incendiary from the start:

"   What's the matter, you dissentious rogues
That, rubbing the poor itch of your opinion,
Make yourselves scabs?" (Ii)

These "fragments" (Ii) live down to his expectations when they refuse to follow him into battle through the gates of Corioles:

"You shames of Rome! You herd of — boils and plagues
Plaster you o'er…" (Iiv)

He is temporarily lost for words.

Coriolanus is a maverick, speaking his mind where others would
wish him to be more diplomatic:

"   His heart's his mouth.
What his breast forges, that his tongue must vent." (IIIi)

(Benedick has a similar character trait in *Much Ado About
Nothing* —

"He hath a heart as sound as a bell, and his tongue is the
clapper: for what his heart thinks his tongue speaks" (IIIii) —

but it doesn't have the same cataclysmic repercussions.)

You give Coriolanus Lear-like, Timon-like stubbornness,
"stoutness" (Vvi). When he refuses to show humility before the
people when he stands for consul,

"   He is banished,
As enemy to the people and his country." (IIIiii)

But his disgust with "The common file" (Ivi) overflows and he
magnificently turns the tables on his "cankered country" (IVv):

"   *I* banish *you*!
                              … Thus I turn my back.
There is a world elsewhere." (IIIiii)

This is universal. This isn't slavish new historicism. But it is
universal because it is rooted in the particular.

Yours,

Nicholas Cobblestone

Dean of the Faculty of Thought

July 8th '08

Dear Mr Shakespeare,

CORIOLANUS

Aufidius' servants take a low view of peace:

SECOND SERVANT   This peace is nothing but to rust iron,
increase tailors, and breed ballad-makers.

FIRST SERVANT   Let me have war, say I. It exceeds peace as
day does night: it's sprightly walking, audible,
and full of vent. Peace is a very apoplexy,
lethargy; mulled, deaf, sleepy, insensible; a
getter of more bastard children than war's a
destroyer of men. (IVv)

The way you voice such approval of war is uncanny!

Best wishes,

Dr Chris Cole

Centre for Peace Studies in Literary Politics

◇◇

June 5th '08

Dear William,

PERICLES

I was concerned that you seemed to be getting nowhere fast
with *Pericles, Prince of Tyre*, so I've had an idea. You know this
hell-raising artist who earns money as a 'victualler', but I suspect
is really a pimp and brothel keeper: George Wilkins? What he
lacks in elegance, he makes up for in passionate humours.
There's real fire in his belly. And I think he'll bring to your writing
what audiences felt was lacking in *Measure for Measure*: that
common touch that made Marston's *The Dutch Courtesan* and
Middleton & Dekker's two-parter *The Honest Whore* such smash-
hits. (I think *Measure* was just a bit too political and serious and

sexually uptight for the debauched times, don't you?) Wilkins will rough you up a bit. He is an occasional writer, as you know – his commercial no-brainer, *The Miseries of Enforced Marriage*, based on that extraordinary case in Yorkshire of the drunken father's double-murder of his kids because of the way his wife treated him (Wilkins ain't a feminist) is proving to be box office gold dust (more than *A Yorkshire Tragedy*...). I think he's just the kick up the backside you need.

Best wishes,

Luke Strong

Artistic Director & Chief Executive

◇◇

July 7th '08

William –

Apologies! I should have known George was your London neighbour. I'm sure you'll get along famously.

Luke

◇◇

September 23rd '08

Dear William,

I was very sorry to hear about your Mother passing away. I know you had a distant relationship with her; but if she ever got to the theatre she would have died happy having seen your relationship reconciled by proxy between Coriolanus and Volumnia towards the end of *Coriolanus*: "O my mother, mother. O!" (Viii).

My condolences.

Luke Strong

Artistic Director & Chief Executive

November 11ᵗʰ '08

Dear William,

PERICLES

The only scene you've written set in a brothel – influenced by your collaboration with Wilkins, no doubt – confounds the brief to be bawdy! It starts well with the Bawd's appropriately disgusting concern that her three whores

> **"with continual action, are even as good as rotten." (IVii)**

But when things could perk up with the purchase of the virginal Marina from the pirates, it goes all flaccid!:

> **"Fie upon her! She's able to freeze the god Priapus and undo a whole generation." (IVii)**

Pull the other one!

Yours,

Lionel Farthing

Executive Associate

◇◇

December 13ᵗʰ '08

Dear William,

PERICLES

I suppose it's the nature of the beast: pairing you with George Wilkins has made the play broken-backed. It really only takes off when his first two acts are over and you announce your three to come by rumbling up the tempest at sea which delivers Pericles a daughter but loses him a wife (IIIi). Yet I am surprised that you haven't managed to be less episodic, less picaresque thereafter. I appreciate that you're using the form significantly, exhausting Pericles on a huge journey around the Mediterranean before his eventual reunion with wife and daughter; but it's an odd way to approach a Romance, if you don't mind me saying so.

I do hope, however, that you will persevere in future plays with attempting to breathe new life into the form. I liked the nods in the direction of Romance that you made a while ago now in *The Comedy of Errors* and, to a certain extent, *Twelfth Night*, and have always felt that there was more mileage for you in sea voyages and tempests, lost children and apparent resurrection.

I particularly like your notion that the daughter is responsible for the rebirth of the father:

"Thou that beget'st him that did thee beget." (Vi)

There won't be a dry eye in the house after that scene, given what we have endured with Pericles throughout the play to this point. This scene is like the "very foolish, fond old man", Lear, being reconciled with his youngest daughter, Cordelia (IVvii).

It is right, isn't it, that in learning from our children we must show more humility in our attempts to impose, parental authority – which Lear and Pericles learn *in extremis*. Children are a check to parental mores and ridiculousnesses – if only to point out when, and how often, we are being wallies. Especially daughters to dads.

Best wishes,

Horatio J. Dowden-Adams

Dramaturg & Associate Producer & Dad to Daughters

◇◇

December 20th '08

Dear William,

"From ashes, ancient Gower is come…"
(Prologue, *Pericles*)

I take my hat off to you: basing *Pericles* in Gower's medieval waffle of stories *Confessio Amantis* is inspired, if a little masochistic. I had to wade through all that guff at University! Bet you're glad you steered well clear of higher education.

Is Gower the only historical fellow poet you present in any of your plays? You ducked out of wheeling on Chaucer in *Richard II*. Cicero is in *Julius Caesar*, but he's a philosopher. If you had a mind to, you could have brought on Homer in *Troilus & Cressida*. Although that would have been a bit tacky.

Best,

Horatio J. Dowden-Adams

◇◇

May 4th '09

Dear William,

I don't know what to say. Wilkins is a complete shyster. First he novelises the play, calling it *The Painfull Adventures of Pericles*. Now he's rumoured to be trying to publish an unauthorised Quarto edition of your jointly-authored play. Sorry.

Yours,

Luke Strong

Artistic Director & Chief Executive

◇◇

November 17th '08

Dear Bill,

Yes I had noticed Thomas Heywood had a play called *The Rape of Lucrece* in production. Don't be angry – be flattered!

Best wishes,

Manfred Mild, Publisher

December 12th '08

Dear William,

A moral victory! What a thrill it must have been to pick up your copy of the fourth Quarto of *Richard II* from Mathew Law's "shop in Paules Church-yard at the signe of the Foxe" and read the title page:

> "The Tragedie of King Richard the Second: With new additions of the Parliament Sceane, and the deposing of King Richard".

These "new additions" are some 163 lines from Bolingbroke's

> "May it please you, lords, to grant the commons' suit?";

to Richard's

> "   Conveyers are you all
> That rise thus nimbly by a true king's fall." (IV)

At last! The Queen is dead: long live the King!

All the best,

Manfred Mild

◇◇

December 13th '08

Dear William,

You didn't write *The Birth of Merlin*, did you? With William Rowley? If not, you should! Or something like it. The Arthurian legend is a great national epic; and you did have the Fool allude to Merlin in *King Lear*, with:

> "This prophesy Merlin shall make, for I live before his time." (IIIii)

Best wishes,

Horatio J. Dowden-Adams

Dramaturg & Associate Producer

May 29th '09

Dear William,

Can I be the first to congratulate you on the publication of your *Sonnets* – at long last. They've been so long in coming that I was beginning to worry that they had gone out of fashion! The vogue in which the heroic Sidney went around sonneteering, almost died out with the Queen. I suspected the publisher, Thomas Thorpe, was indulging you in a bit of vanity publishing, a bit of quaint Elizabethan nostalgia in this wicked Jacobean age. And it's true that on the surface they're crammed with similar Petrarchan and anti-Petrarchan sentiment from a poet-lover persona. But where your Elizabethan forbears wrote their sequences as a kind of 'complaint', which included a literary quarrel, your concern is more to tease out the real image of the person you are writing to (and for?). Your *Sonnets* will create their own fashion. Indeed, they are beyond fashion, reinventing the form.

The correlation between your plays and your sonnets is amazing, and even though I have read these sonnets in manuscript over the past fifteen years or so – as Francis Meres' fleetingly reported in *Palladis Tamia*, his 700 page-long pensées on the contemporary literary scene (1598), as your "sugared sonnets among his private friends" – I find it rewarding to read them as a collection. It's a terrific achievement.

All my love,

Luke Strong

Artistic Director

P.S. *A Lover's Complaint* which is published as a coda to the *Sonnets*: when did you write this?

June 1st '09

Dear William,

THE SONNETS

Your *Sonnets* are clearly deeply personal while at the same time being self-consciously universal. Your *Sonnets* are also artfully equivocal as to whether you are the poet-lover, or whether this is just a useful role to adopt as a conceit. The range of emotion is astonishing.

You can do this because of the seeming paradox of the liberating strictures of your form: three ten syllable (iambic pentameter) quatrains followed by one couplet, which consolidates/contradicts:

-/-/-/-/-A

-/-/-/-/-B

-/-/-/-/-A

-/-/-/-/-B

-/-/-/-/-C

-/-/-/-/-D

-/-/-/-/-C

-/-/-/-/-D

-/-/-/-/-E

-/-/-/-/-F

-/-/-/-/-E

-/-/-/-/-F

-/-/-/-/-G

-/-/-/-/-G

These poems are a living metaphor for your poetic and dramatic art which will be your legacy. Your spirit will live on eternally in the re-creation of your work once your mortal body is a worm-ridden corpse.

You berate time for ageing your lover:

"Nor draw no lines there with thine antique pen." (19)

Yet you say you can defeat time:

"His beauty shall in these black lines be seen,
And they shall live, and he in them still green." (63)

On the other hand, you do, on occasion, modestly acknowledge your present inadequacies:

"   You yourself, being extant, well might show
How far a modern quill doth come too short." (83)

This is false modesty, William. You are well aware that you write with a "modern quill" (83), not an "antique pen" (19). In immortalising your love, you have ensured the immutability of your sonnets.

Best wishes,

Horatio J. Dowden Adams

Dramaturg & Associate Producer

◇◇

June 15th '09

Dear William,

WILLIAM SHAKESPEARE: THE SONNETS

Did you write the poems to be read in one's head? Or read aloud? And if the latter, to oneself? Or to a private audience? And if the latter, why not to a public audience?! Each one is a mini-drama.

I've got a suggestion: let's develop your *Sonnets* into a dramatised performance: WILLIAM SHAKESPEARE: THE SONNETS. We'll stage them! Here's what I have in mind:

We'll take Sonnet 23 as our cue:

> "As an imperfect actor on the stage
> Who with his fear is put besides his part..."

And then he stumbles, fumbles for the lines, repeats them, but can get no further – because he is overwhelmed by his love! So we trot through a selection of sonnets in a three-act drama, thus:

Act I

15: "This huge stage presenteth nought but shows"

17: "Live twice – in it and in my rhyme"

18: "Shall I compare thee to a summer's day"

20: "The Master/Mistress of my passion"

23: "As an imperfect actor on the stage"

27: "Weary with toil I haste me to my bed"

29: "Haply I think on thee"   [sleep?]

Act II

33: "Glorious morning!"

34: "Why didst thou promise such a beauteous day?"
                              [drizzle/umbrella?]

35: "Civil war is in my love and hate"

60: "So do our minutes hasten to their end"

63: "His beauty shall in these black lines be seen"

71: "No longer mourn for me when I am dead"   [anger]

73: "In me thou seest the twilight of such day"

[interval?]

Act III

76:   "You and love are still my argument"

94:   "Lords and masters of their faces"

112: "All the world besides methinks are dead"

115: "Love is a babe"

116: "Let me not to the marriage of true minds"

126: "O, thou, my lovely boy"

129: "Th'expense of spirit in a waste of shame"

130: "My mistress' eyes are nothing like the sun"

138: "Love's best habit is in seeming trust"

139: "Kill me outright with looks and rid my pain"

141: "I do not love thee with mine eyes"

144: "Two loves I have"   [fair man/dark lady]

145: "'I hate' from hate away she threw"

147: "My love is as a fever longing still"

151: "Rising at thy name doth point out thee"   [erection]

154: "Love's fire heats water, water cools not love"

[as a finale song]

One actor, but the two lovers projected on stage in some way?
I'm really excited by this. It will get me back into the rehearsal
room.

What do you think?

Best wishes,

Luke Strong

Artistic Director & Executive Chairman Designate

July 12th '09

Dear William,

SONNETS

You can be too maudlin sometimes:

> "Alas, 'tis true I have gone here and there
> And made myself a motley to the view,
> Gored mine own thoughts, sold cheap what is most dear,
> Made old offences of affections new.
> Most true it is that I have looked on truth
> Askance and strangely…" (110)

I don't see much evidence of you cheaply 'selling out' in your writing, or goring your ideas and making too many compromises. You are a writer of integrity. Keep looking "on truth askance and strangely". It's what you do best and what we love you for.

Best wishes,

Luke Strong

◇◇

August 18th '09

Dear William,

SONNETS

I understand that Thomas Thorpe may have pulled a fast one in publishing your *Sonnets* and that you may not be too happy about it after all. I guess Anne won't be overjoyed by their appearance, dredging up the rumours about you and the Earl of Southampton again:

> "   …The Master-Mistress of my passion …
> …She pricked thee out for woman's pleasure."
> (20)

I also don't think Anne will be pacified with the inclusion of your insipid juvenilia sonnet – the only one in the entire sequence with eight, not ten syllable lines – with its private joke with Anne Shakespeare, née Hath-away:

> "'I hate' from **hate away** she threw,
> And saved my life, saying 'not you'." (145)

And when from Sonnet 127 you change gear and start addressing a new love in your torrid masterpieces...who is this Dark Lady? Anne will be livid. You're 45; Anne, 53. Don't make a fool of yourself with "th'uncertain sickly appetite" (147) of love-lust:

> "Th'expense of spirit in a waste of shame
> Is lust in action..." (129)

Lust is a potent and chaotic experience, unmanageable in its feverish intensity. (This is Angelo's experience in *Measure for Measure*: policing a city stewed in lust, he is overcome by it, crazed by a physical passion he has intellectually rejected.)

Superb writing. But it won't be good for your steadfast relationship.

Yours in friendship,

Richard B'Age

◇◇

September 19th '09

Dear William,

SONNET 138

Your brilliant parody of conventional Petrarchan love poetry – which you have done before, of course, not least you with Romeo beating off about Rosaline before he meets Juliet – is a *tour de force*. It is a <u>real</u> love poem, to the Dark Lady (who *is* she?) – a world away from the merry:

> "*Shall* I compare thee to a summer's day?
> Thou art *more* lovely and more temperate." (12)

And yet this mature love almost turns cynical in the mutual self-deceptions and punning "lies" (untruths and sex):

> "When my love swears that she is made of truth,
> I do believe her, though I know she lies...
> O, love's best habit is in seeming trust...
> Therefore I lie with her, and she with me,
> And in our faults by lies we flattered be." (138)

It's just struck me that this isn't to the Other Woman at all. The Dark Lady is Anne, isn't she?

Much love,

Luke Strong

◇◇

MEMO

October 16th '10

From: Horatio

To: Luke

Re: CYMBELINE

Shakespeare has taken the seething sexuality and jealousy and lust from *Othello* and from *Measure for Measure*, and from his *Sonnets*, and bound it all up in this emerging form of a tragi-comic romance.

When Iachimo creeps into Imogen's bedroom while she sleeps, he sees

> "   She hath been reading late:
> The tale of Tereus – here the leaf's turn'd down." (IIii)

This is the very tale which inspired *Titus Andronicus* all those years ago. But Iachimo doesn't rape or mutilate Imogen physically. He does so symbolically. He gathers intimate details to report to her husband, Posthumus, so that Posthumus' faith in his wife's fidelity is undermined, his self-centred jealousy aroused, his egocentric sense of honour flouted – like in all those plays that Shakespeare's Spanish contemporaries are writing, where men feel their honour shamed because their sister/daughter/wife's honour is violently abused.

Posthumus is sexually possessive of Imogen from the start, calling her "My queen, my mistress" (Ii) with all its overtones of licentiousness. With greater humility, and more dignity, and truer love, he overflows with emotion when reunited with her at the end of the play:

> "My queen, my life, my wife, O Imogen,
> Imogen, Imogen!" (Vv)

He also condemns her to bondage with a ring and a bracelet:

> "   For my sake wear this:
> It is the manacle of love." (Iii)

She is imprisoned, enslaved by his attempts to own her, to control her. It is this paranoia in Posthumus that Iachimo gleefully feeds upon.

In Imogen's bedroom, as she sleeps, there is a creepy visual moment where Iachimo emerges from a trunk and notes the circumstantial details with which to torment Posthumus:

> "   On her left breast
> A mole cinque-spotted… This secret
> Will force him think I have picked the lock and ta'en
> The treasure of her honour." (IIii)

Which it does. Posthumus lashes out at Imogen in her absence, first against her frigidity:

> "Me of my lawful pleasure she restrained
> And prayed me oft forbearance: did it with
> A pudency so rosy…that I thought her
> As chaste as unsunned snow." (IIiv)

He then pictures Iachimo rutting Imogen:

> "Like a full-acorned boar, a German one,
> Cried 'O!' and mounted." (IIiv)

And from this dark place of tawdry imaginings he fulminates against women:

> "   There's no motion
> That tends to vice in man, but I affirm
> It is the woman's part: be it lying, note it,
> The woman's; flattering, hers; deceiving, hers;
> Lust and rank thoughts, hers; revenge, hers;
> Ambitions, covetings, change of prides, disdain,
> Nice longing, slanders, mutability –
> All faults that name, nay, that hell knows, why, hers."
>
> (IIiv)

But his show of dark, misogynist anger in the short phrases and rapid thoughts and puffed out repetition of "hers", betrays a deeper self-loathing and sense of his own inadequacy as a man. And shows him to be gullible – like virtually everyone in this play: Cymbeline, Cloten, Imogen; even her long-lost brothers.

Shakespeare draws on Fletcher and Beaumont's tragi-comic, court-pastoral romances like last year's *Philaster, or Love Lies A-Bleeding*, as well as his own past plays. There are elements of King Lear in the stubborn blindness of King Cymbeline, and also in the primitivism of pagan Britain which glorifies the gods, especially Jupiter (who appears *deus ex machina* (Viv)): "Heaven mend all!" entreats Cymbeline – and he is immediately rewarded by the entrance of Imogen, now a Roman slave. There are echoes of *As You Like It* (and *The Two Gentlemen of Verona*) with Imogen disguising herself as the boy Fidele in her retreat into the Welsh valleys above Milford Haven. Imogen in disguise learns what it is to be male:

> "I see a man's life is a tedious one." (IIIvi)

At the same time, Shakespeare looks into the potential future of drama. There's a supreme moment of clash of tastes and styles when Imogen, whom we've all thought to be dead, awakes, like Juliet in the tomb, alongside Cloten's headless, disguised trunk, which she believes it to be the corpse of Posthumus –

"A headless man? The garments of Posthumus?" (IVii)

It's the height of bad-taste black-humour, a perverse comic device, grotesque, absurd; yet her mistaken mourning is very moving. It demonstrates the unconditionality of her love.

In Imogen, Shakespeare has created a lovely woman – idealised? I don't think so. But he has shown that the men around her – father, husband, would-be lovers – are not worthy of her.

Horatio

◇◇◇

MEMO

March 12th '11

To: Luke

From: Horatio

Re: THE WINTER'S TALE

In all of Shakespeare's work the contradictory co-exists, simultaneously. This is the essence of the antitheses of his stories, his characters, his structure, his language.

This is not, however, unique to Shakespeare; though it is stronger in his work than in his contemporaries'. It is a legacy of the fluidity and sheer capacity of the medieval mind, which thrived in a state of flux, where worlds weren't compartmentalised and differentiated as they are now in the mind-set of our finicky, Western psychologies, where we are constantly battling to impose restrictive order on the untamed, untamable world. Shakespeare's world is more Eastern, in a way, freer, where sacred and secular, God and gods co-mingle, Western European sensibilities reverberating with the philosophies of Asia and the Orient. Dualities can be reconciled in the world of his plays in contrast to how we, in our private and public life, are determined to seek out difference and confrontation.

Take the moment in *The Winter's Tale* where Hermione's true-to-life statue is revealed– itself an echo of the 'resurrection' of

> "The former Hero! Hero that is dead!" (*Much Ado*, Viv):
> "The fixture of her eye has motion in't,
> As we are mocked with art." (*Winter's Tale*, Viii)

Then:

> "   It is required
> You do awake your faith" (Viii) –

us, as well as the characters on stage. And then the 'statue' "stirs":

> "   O, she's warm!
> If this be magic, let it be an art
> Lawful as eating." (Viii)

Is this magic? Is this a religious experience? Is this "an old tale" (Viii)? Is this a con-trick, sixteen years in the making, or has Hermione been in a trance, suspended animation, a coma? Or has she been in contemplative retreat, like Thaisa in *Pericles*, all these years?

To all these questions, yes. And more. We are disbelieving, yet we suspend our disbelief, caught up in the moment and wanting, needing to believe. In performance we sense, feel, know, understand, believe and disbelieve all at the same time. In the same way a Hindu believes in the living god when making *puja* offerings at its temple icon, in the coconut-oil lamplight and incense-infused, sweet ghee-smelling, heady atmosphere as part of *Darshan* (literally 'seeing') – and yet knows the icon is only a representation of a god. In the same way as the physical metamorphoses of Ovid are conceivable *in extremis* – and yet we know they are merely a symbol for psychological transformation. And in the same way as we have inherited in Christianity the belief in the transubstantiation of the bread and wine into Christ's flesh and blood in the act of communion – and yet know it does not really alter to turn us cannibal.

The spiritual experience of *The Winter's Tale* is overwhelming. Hermione's language of reconciliation with her lost daughter, Perdita (the simultaneously royal and rustic "queen of curds and cream" (IViv)), is highly ritualised:

> "   You gods look down,
> And from your sacred vials pour your graces
> Upon my daughter's head!" (Viii)

Leontes has vowed:

> "   Once a day I'll visit
> The chapel where they lie, and tears shed there
> Shall be my recreation." (IIIii)

Recreation as in pastime and re-creation. All these spiritual themes have their basis not in manmade religions or even ancient myths, but from long before these artificial conceits: from nature and from time.

Time literally appears in *The Winter's Tale*, as simultaneous epilogue to the first half, prologue to the second. In *Macbeth*, time brings oblivion:

> "Creeps in this petty pace from day to day
> To the last syllable of recorded time." (*Macbeth*, Vv)

In *Hamlet*, time was tortured on the rack:

> "The time is out of joint." (*Hamlet*, Iv)

Similarly, in *Twelfth Night*, written at the same time as *Hamlet*:

> "How have the hours racked and tortured me." (*12N*, V)

Also in *Twelfth Night*, time is an irrepressible, mechanical, spinning top:

> "Thus the whirligig of time brings in his revenges."
> *(12N,* V)

In *Love's Labour's Lost* it is "cormorant devouring time" (*LLL,* Ii), as it is in *Richard II*:

> "I wasted time and now doth time waste me." (*RII,* Vv)

In *Othello*, time gestates:

> "There are many events in the womb of time which will be delivered" (*Oth,* Iiii)

But in *The Winter's Tale*, Time brings truth and reconciliation, redemption and resurrection.

In the heroic couplets of Time's "swift passage" (IVi), I hear an authorial voice – and I suspect Shakespeare has written the part of Time for himself, like the Chorus in *Henry V.* Time and the author are the interchangeable "I":

> "   Impute it not a crime
> To me, or my swift passage, that I slide
> O'er sixteen years... "(IVi)

There is a sense of divine, omnipotent, authorial control in the telling of "my tale" and appealing to us "Gentle spectators" (IVi):

> "I turn my glass and give my scene such growing
> As you had slept between." (IVi)

(Presumably we want the interval just before this?)

The Winter's Tale shares Shakespeare's comedic, rural play-grounds/testing-grounds, book-ended with the political and moral authority of state power, of *A Midsummer Night's Dream* or *As You Like It.* There are similar journeys in his History Plays, where test in battle and anarchic subversion are the equivalent of his rural retreats. If they aren't as convincingly completed as they are in his Romances, then that's because in real life, as history shows us in magnification, our achievements fall short of our aspirations; our aims are thwarted, and we all muddle along. Perhaps the Romances have a calmer sense of Karma, where we go further by allowing things to happen to us, by being passive. By being active, as in the Histories, and trying to determine our futures, life just explodes in our faces.

Horatio

◇◇

April 2nd '11

Dear William,

THE WINTER'S TALE

You're both modern and old-fashioned in *The Winter's Tale*. Modern, because you're nothing if not innovative. Old-fashioned because you've dramatised Robert Greene's prose Romance *Pandosto: The Triumph of Time*.

Greene! Who did so much from beyond the grave to undermine the promising young playwright "Shake-scene". Are you shake-shafting him some twenty years on? You have triumphed in time over his sort, that condescending "college of wit-crackers" as you called them in *Much Ado About Nothing* (Viv).

Your play starts in the present (with a brief retrospective "recoil" of 23 years to Leontes' boyhood (Iii)) and then jumps forward sixteen years. And each half of the play begins in the same manner: with Camillo, in prose, giving us a low-key low-down on the present situation. But William: terrible carelessness! Camillo says:

"It is *fifteen* years since I saw my country." (IVii)

Time has just told us it's "sixteen years" (IVi). Make your mind up!

Actually, your play is riddled with inconsistencies. For example:

"   Our ship hath touched upon
The deserts of Bohemia." (IIIiii)

Bohemia is landlocked. It's at the very heart of continental Europe, its geographic epicentre, just as your native Warwickshire (into which Bohemia quickly mutates) is coast-less in the Mid-lands of England, further from the sea in any direction than any other county.

However, I don't have a problem with your anachronisms – I never have in your plays. Given that your preferred mode of production is modern-dress, and that the plays are set simultaneously in the time in which they're set and in your own time, the circumstantial detail of the 16th century artist Julio Romano being the supposed painter of the Hermione statue, is fine by me (Vii).

You use the ingredients of familiar fables told to pass the hours on chilly winter evenings:

- Noble children, abandoned "where chance may nurse or end it" (IIiii)
- Parental opposition to a child's inappropriate choice of love-match (IViv)
- Rural customs and summer harvests (IViv)

Played as dramatised fairy tale, the fantastical outcomes of the story even confound the popular press' hunger for sensation:

"Such a deal of wonder is broken out within this hour that ballad-makers cannot be able to express it… This news, which is called true, is so like an old tale that the verity of it is in strong suspicion." (Vii)

This actually defuses our incredulity – we never for a moment think it is escapist confection.

What we see and hear in *The Winter's Tale* – *the* ultimate winter's tale to triumph over all other winter's tales – is a story of such truth that we are moved to our very core.

With very best wishes,

Luke Strong

Artistic Director & Executive Chairman

◊◊◊

April 15th '11

Dear William,

THE WINTER'S TALE

I thought you'd written all-consuming sexual jealousy out of your system – in *Othello*, *Measure for Measure*, even in the part of Ford in *The Merry Wives of Windsor*. But here you are again dredging up your most frightening morbidity in Leontes:

"   She has been sluiced in his absence
And his pond fished by his next neighbour." (*WT*, Iii)

Pompey Bum in *Measure for Measure* only quipped about "groping for trouts in a peculiar river" (*Measure*, Iii). Leontes is darkly obsessed. He needs therapy.

But I guess you're okay if you're able to exorcise your demons through writing.

Yours,

Luke Strong

May 5th '11

Dear Mr Shakespeare,

"Exit, pursued by a bear" (*WT*, IIIiii) must be the most memorable stage direction ever written! Especially because you're so sparing with them as a rule. And anticipating it at the performance of *The Winter's Tale* last night (for all the bright ideas about doubling the bear with Hermione) I was expecting a Paris Gardens, bear-baiting pit-bear to trundle on, as it did in *Mucedorus*. So the polar bear cub was a *coup de théâtre*!

Best wishes,

Loren Spiegelei

Literary Department

◇◇

July 7th '11

Dear Will,

THE TEMPEST

I don't know if you've spotted this trend in theatre lately: the more the veteran critics plead for the survival of the solo-authored, autonomous, well-made, state-of-the-nation play in the lyric playhouse, the more the younger generation of theatre-makers devise pieces in found spaces in defiant acts of creative collaboration. The more the older generation expresses its distrust of youthful adaptations, the more those adaptors are recognised by the rest of the theatre establishment as proper playwrights, winning prizes usually reserved for 'original' writers. Which is great news for you. Almost every one of your plays has been an adaptation (apart from *Merry Wives* and *Love's Labour's Lost*).

I'm not sure how you'd feel about abandoning the playhouse for an industrial, site-specific location, but I know you're flexible: outdoor theatres; found spaces within pre-existing indoor spaces like Blackfriars; making do with the Inns at Court; the royal command performances at the palaces; the country house gigs; and of course coxing and boxing your way around these Isles on tour.

So, in this context, I think your last play, your personal project, your love letter/suicide note to British Theatre – I mean, of course, *The Tempest* – is a kind of one-man show taking place inside Prospero's head. The story of this exiled magician-philosopher-King marooned on an island is self-reflective. It follows on from those lost-children-all-at-sea themes of your late plays *Pericles*, *Cymbeline* and *The Winter's Tale*, as well as harping back to *Twelfth Night* and even earlier, to *The Comedy of Errors*.

And yet *The Tempest* has got more razzmatazz than all of them put together. With its song-and-dance numbers, its pair of clowns, its shipwreck live on-stage (at least in *Twelfth Night* it was *off*-), *The Tempest* is very show-biz! And you've thrown in a bit of love interest and a noble savage. You're trying to cram it all in as a last hurrah, aren't you?

I think the time is ripe for you, the grumpy old fuddy-duddy of the theatre, about to retire to the country, to show the emerging artists that you're the most experimental of the lot.

Best wishes,

Luke Strong

Artistic Director & Executive Chair

P.S. And because it is sourced from a letter (William Strachey's *True Reportory of the Wracke*, 15th July 1610) and a translated essay (John Florio's version of Montaigne's *Of the Caniballes*, 1603, which itself draws on Ovid's *Metamorphoses*), it should get nominated for all those 'original' play prizes!

MEMO

July 8th '11

From: Horatio

To: Loren

Re: THE TEMPEST

The Tempest is a discourse on Art: the art of government, of playwriting, of magic. Discuss.

The Tempest is a discourse on Colonialism. Discuss.

Horatio

◇◇

July 10th '11

Dear William,

THE TEMPEST

Not since *Twelfth Night* have you written such a technically perfect play.

Were you aware that *The Tempest* is the second shortest of all your plays, *The Comedy of Errors* being the shortest? Were you also aware that they're the two plays of yours that come closest to obeying the Aristotelian Unities of Time, Place and Action? *Othello* comes close-ish after the first act. *A Midsummer Night's Dream* has a good go between its book-end acts.

Best wishes,

Horatio J. Dowden-Adams

Dramaturg & Associate Producer

P.S. *Hamlet*, then *Richard III* are your longest plays.

August 20th '11

Dear William,

THE TEMPEST

Lost children, particularly daughters, are found throughout your work – lost to fathers, mainly, though the Abbess in *The Comedy of Errors*, Constance in *King John*, Thaisa in *Pericles* and Hermione in *The Winter's Tale* are honourable mother exceptions. We can make much of the death of Hamnet, and conjecture that the childhood of your two surviving daughters, now in their mid-twenties, has also been lost to you while you've been beavering away in London. These late plays in particular are love letters from fathers to daughters, asking forgiveness for absence but also asking for understanding if you have behaved tyrannically towards them when you were there.

In *The Tempest*, Prospero learns to be a father, as much as anything else, to be responsible for all in his charge: Miranda, Ariel, Caliban, Ferdinand, the state of Milan – the welding of good husbandry to good parenting. He wilfully tears families apart in order to reconstruct them. But only when he releases his charges does he learn the last rite of passage of parenthood.

Yours,

Luke Strong

◇◇

August 8th '11

Dear William,

THE TEMPEST

Your courtiers are on the return leg of their journey from "Afric" from "the marriage of the King's fair daughter Claribel to the King of Tunis" (Iii). So I'd say the island is in the Mediterranean rather than the Atlantic. It is not a Utopia but a testing-ground, like Arden in *As You Like It*, or the woods in *The Two Gentlemen* of *Verona* and *A Midsummer Night's Dream*, or England is for Malcolm in *Macbeth*, and even Petruchio's cold house is for hot-headed Kate in *The Taming of the Shrew*. We leave home to learn about ourselves, like Christ in the wilderness, like Bolingbroke, anyone really, on a pilgrimage; then we can return better people.

London has been your island. You now return to Stratford, duking it in your own realm.

Yours,

Luke Strong

◇◇◇

September 9th '11

Dear William,

THE TEMPEST

Is this your last play? Have you finally laid the ghost of Christopher Marlowe to rest?

In Marlowe's last play, *Doctor Faustus*, Faustus is surrounded by books, "ravished" (Ii) by them. He practices black magic.

In *The Tempest*, Prospero has been furnished with "volumes that I prize above my kingdom" from his own library (Iii). He practices white magic.

Faustus tries to repent: "I'll burn my books." (Vii)

Prospero revokes, repents, is redeemed: "I'll drown my book." (V)

"Faustus is gone. Regard his hellish fall…" is Marlowe's Epilogue.

"Let your indulgence set me free" is yours.

And as we release Prospero from the confines of the play, we may well reflect that in the battle between Kit and Will, you just about won. In the end.

"We are such stuff as dreams are made on…" (IV)

Horatio

<hr>

January 19th '12

Dear William,

DON QUIXOTE

Miguel Cervantes' *Don Quixote* is a best-selling blockbuster. At its heart it tells the story of a disillusioned former chivalric knight tilting at windmills in delusions of grandeur, supported by his faithful servant Sancho Panza. It is very you. You should adapt it for the theatre.

You'll probably want a co-writer – it's a big book. John Fletcher, your successor as the King's Men's in-house dramatist (or 'Ordinary Poet' as was your customary job title) might be up for it. It's good to look to the younger generation to keep our ideas and ideals refreshed. I know you had misgivings about his *Taming of the Shrew* sequel *The Woman's Prize or The Tamer Tamed (or The Taming of the Tamer)*. But isn't imitation the greatest form of flattery? And his play has revived interest in your Elizabethan juvenilia. (By the way, did you do *The Taming of A Shrew* that's still also doing the rounds some twenty years on? It bears a remarkable semblance to *The Shrew*, except with a few extra Sly scenes.)

I don't expect you've read Cervantes' original Spanish, but Book One has just been translated. What do you think?

Best wishes,

Luke Strong

February 18th '12

Dear William,

CARDENIO

I'm so glad you and Fletcher have hit it off. His is a precocious talent which will go far, I'm sure.

I am surprised but pleased that you have both run with the idea of taking the relatively minor episode of Cardenio from *Don Quixote* and turning it into a fully-fledged tragi-comedy in the manner of your Spanish contemporary, Lope de Vega. By pairing Cardenio's insanity (because he's betrayed in his love for Lucinda by the conniving Don Fernando) with the funny cross-dressing episode of Dorotea (disguising herself as a man because she's ashamed to have allowed herself to be coerced into having sex with a rich man's son) you'll create a great double-act – like Beatrice and Benedick in *Much Ado*.

Emulating your Spanish contemporaries is appropriate for the material – and wise, given the success of their plays. Did you know that the plays in Spain are so popular that profits from performances are used by the authorities to subsidise the hospitals? Now there's an incentive for State funding of the arts if ever there was one!

Best wishes,

Luke Strong

◇◇

April 24th '12

Dear William and John,

CARDENIO

Such are the vagaries of the internal post that between my office and Horatio's we've managed to lose our script of *Cardenio*. I hope it wasn't your only copy!

Luke

October 28ᵗʰ '12

William –

The sudden death of Prince Henry is a blow. King James and the Court will be distraught. We all had high hopes for him as a future king and enthusiastic patron of the Arts. Still, we will have to see how Charles now fairs as heir. He seems to have a good head on his shoulders.

Best,

Lionel Farthing

◇◇

MEMO

April 9ᵗʰ '13

From: Horatio

To: Luke

ALL IS TRUE: THE FAMOUS HISTORY OF THE LIFE OF KING HENRY EIGHTH

It seems a paradox, but fiction can be truer than fact. "The fact of the matter" bleated by politicians of all persuasions, always alerts us to party political prejudice, to manipulative propaganda. Story-telling, the telling of tales, alerts us to passionate truths.

What Bill and John both seem to be driving at in their new history play about Henry VIII's divorce from Katharine of Aragon and his hasty marriage to Anne Boleyn, is that truth is too often a matter for polarising conjecture.

I've heard Christian heads of state proclaim:

"You're either with us; or you're against us".

Just because we don't agree with their sabre-rattling crusades, doesn't make us their enemy! But in a world of polarisation, one man's truth is another man's lies – and vice versa. It's the fundamental problem of the fundamentalists of all political and religious hues. There is no entertaining the notion that there might be another, middle way, or, indeed, a radical alternative.

In early 16th century England the opposing factions were at loggerheads. At the beginning of that century, the state religion was Catholicism. When Henry VIII needed to determine his own future and not be in hock to Rome, he broke with the Catholics, and thus risked political isolation by forging a new kind of English Protestantism with his own politically expedient, Lutheranesque Reformation – what his Catholic opponents dismissed as "this new sect" (*HVIII*, Vii). However, Shakespeare and Fletcher both seem to blame the roving eye of a middle-aged man. Is Henry's Reformation sparked by religious/political imperatives? By the desperation for a male heir? No: lust!

Shakespeare's own father was born a Catholic in a Catholic state. Time and history moved on. Fletcher and Shakespeare were born Protestants in a Protestant State. The world of intrigue and conspiracies and spying spilled into the world of playmaking, with Anthony Munday a spy at the Catholic college in Rome; with God knows what shenanigans Marlowe was embroiled in, leading to his untimely demise.

Those on the wrong side of history at any given time are persecuted, tortured, murdered by the State. But sides change. Who's to say that the wrong side won't later become the right side, that the outlawed, treasonous 'terrorist' won't become the next Head of State?

At the height of any paranoia, an enemy is sought to scapegoat; and, where he doesn't exist, he is conjured, his wrongdoings concocted. Take the history of scapegoating suffered by worldwide Jewry. Witness the perpetual appetite for seeking out the enemy within.

All is True is an ambiguous play, deliberately so. It can be played with all the pomp and pageant associated with our inherited view of Holbein's famous portrait of Henry. And it can be played with all that guff, but with a *Verfremdungseffekt* – an estranging, distancing, alienating sense of irony. Or the rulers can be stripped down to human scale, domesticated, intimate. All will be true, up to a point.

For me the truest moments in *All is True* are when the play is spot on with its emotional truth. And this is at its most sublime at the end of the play. It's a tender moment when Henry beholds his new baby daughter Elizabeth:

"   Never before
This happy child did I get anything." (Viv)

Henry has matured – not necessarily as a political leader, but as a man, as a father. All fathers of new daughters have experienced that moment.

Horatio

◇◇◇

30/6/13

Dear William,

Disaster! The Globe burned to the ground. In less than an hour! By a rogue cannon, used for sound fx, discharging itself into the thatched roofing at the beginning of All Is True: Henry VIII.

Thank heavens there are no casualties! The man whose breeches were set on fire looked like he would be boiled alive, until a quick-witted groundling chucked a bottle of ale over him.

In my view it would be best if life moved on and the Globe was never resurrected, don't you think? I'd hate it to become some kind of mausoleum for tribute theatre in years to come. At least give it all mod cons – after all, there wouldn't have been a fire if the roof had been tiled.

If they do go for the full rebuild they should find out which brand of beer saved that man's life. They could get them to sponsor the new theatre.

Yours,

Lionel Farthing

◇◇

July 6th '13

Dear Will,

THE KNIGHT'S TALE

Forgive me for writing so soon after the Globe's cremation. But John Fletcher's come up with a great idea to follow up on your joint success of *All Is True: Henry VIII*.

We're in negotiation with Blackfriars' Theatre – I know indoor public spaces have smaller, more elitist, maler audiences, but think of the stage effects you can employ. We may be able to get Inigo Jones on board.

Like you did in *Troilus & Cressida*, John's looked to Chaucer for inspiration and wants to write about the rivalry between the two young knights, Palamon and Arcite. There's that old Richard Edwards play, *Palamon & Arcite*, from the '60s that Henslowe revived in the '90s. But you'll be most familiar with their story from *The Canterbury Tales' Knight's Tale*, the one that inspired your Theseus and Hippolyta story-line in *A Midsummer Night's Dream*.

John's also got a very sexy idea of his own about having the knights see Emilia in the garden from their prison, just as the

Gaoler's Daughter spots *them* through their prison bars. So the chaste courtly love of Emilia will be contrasted with the highly charged, sexual love of the Gaoler's Daughter. Neat, no?

There's also another kind of love to explore – the love between friends – in Arcite and Palamon's falling out over the same seemingly unattainable girl, Emilia. And all their young love and desires can be seen against the powerful marriage of Theseus to Hippolyta, Emilia's sister.

John also wants the Gaoler's Daughter's love to be unrequited and for her to take her own life, paying homage to Ophelia's death in a way.

Here's "the rub" (as you coined in *Hamlet* (IIIi)). John wants you to write the first Act and the last, sandwiching his young man's energy between your wisdom. And with Blackfriars in mind, he's wondering if you can bring some ritualistic gravitas to it, especially in the person of the sage philosopher-King Theseus. You'll recall that Chaucer has the scenes of devotion in the temples of Venus (Palamon), Mars (Arcite) and Diana (Emilia) before the final show-down. I know you've always been obsessed with the conundrum of why we still believe our fate to be in the hands of the gods rather than with ourselves, so you could use this as an excuse for further reflection.

Old playwrights don't retire. And they shouldn't fade away either. Let me know.

Best wishes,

Luke Strong

Artistic Director Emeritus

3/11/13

Dear Will,

TWO NOBLE KINSMEN

Good title! And John's just delivered a smashing Prologue and Epilogue which I think does justice to your joint venture. As you'd expect from John, it starts suggestively:

> **"New plays and maidenheads are near akin"…**
> **(Prologue, 2NK)**

What does it feel like, at nearly 50, to be losing your virginity all over again with another world première?

I hope to see you at the opening night – let me know if you need picking up from the Stratford Express.

All the best,

Lionel

◇◇

May 3rd '15

Dear Mr Shakespeare,

Thank you for doing us the honour, sir, of being the key-note guest speaker at our Annual General Meeting of the Friends of the Theatre. We were most impressed with your recollections of a life in the theatre and of the eyebrow-raising issues of funding and governance which seem to dog so much of the artist's endeavours nowadays. Your *bon mots*, if I may say so, were thought-provoking and inspiring as ever. And please do thank Mrs Shakespeare for the exquisite canapés.

Yours sincerely,

Reginald Pigginbottom
President
Friends of the Theatre

July 4th '15

Dear William,

It's been suggested that we ditch the John Lyly retrospective and spend next year doing a Festival of your Complete Works. It will steal the thunder from the publication of Ben Jonson's monumental *Works* and will remind everyone that, though you're now past 50, you ain't finished yet.

I'd like to suggest playing all the plays in order – reverse order, i.e. chronologically backwards, starting with *The Two Noble Kinsmen* and ending with *The Taming of the Shrew* (I for one am convinced that you really did write it, though I wish you hadn't!)

In order that they all sell out, we'll say that following this Festival there will be a ten year moratorium on your works. It's a marketing ploy and we wouldn't stick to it if market forces dictate otherwise.

What do you think?

Charity Snicker
Executive Producer Designate

April 26th '16

To the Editor

Dear Sir,

Further to your obituary of William Shakespeare (April 24th '16), we would like to remind the nation, indeed the world, of the last lines Shakespeare ever wrote for the stage: his ending to *The Two Noble Kinsmen*, the final flourish of his rejuvenating partnership with his younger mentee John Fletcher.

Echoing the end of *The Knight's Tale*, by that other great national poet Geoffrey Chaucer, we believe it is a fitting final tribute from the man himself, still curious whether his life was in his own hands or the gods':

"   O you heavenly charmers,
What things you make of us! For what we lack
We laugh; for what we have are sorry; still
Are children in some kind. Let us be thankful
For that which is, and with you leave dispute
That are above our question. Let's go off,
And bear us like the time.   " (Viv)

Significantly, he left that last line short of the final four syllables/two beats which would complete the iambic pentameter of the blank verse line of which he was the master.

His final stage direction is the final stage direction of his own life:

"Flourish. Exeunt   "

No final full stop.

Ripeness is all. The rest is silence.

Yours,

Luke Strong, Horatio J. Dowden-Adams, Lionel Farthing, Bob Castle, Sasha Radish

Producers, Dramaturgs, Directors, Friends

August 8th '18

Dear Mrs. John Hall,

THE WILL

Susannah – I'm glad your father left your mother the "second-best bed" in his will. It would have been the one he shared with her on those rare occasions when he was at home, and it must have sentimental value. The first bed, kept for guests, will serve you and your husband Dr John Hall well at The Croft.

It was also decent of your father to leave 28 shillings and 8 pence each to Richard Burbage, John Heminge and Henry Condell to buy 'rings' to remember him by.

Leaving his estate otherwise to you and eventually to his grand-daughter, Elizabeth, makes good sense. Your poor sister, Judith, marrying the rotter Thomas Quiney in February 1616, only for him to be up on trial a month later for getting another woman pregnant. No wonder William altered his will at the last moment to prevent Judith inheriting a bean – and thus stopping Quiney from getting his hands on any of it. (The fact that the woman in question subsequently died in childbirth, and the baby was stillborn, is tragic.)

Meanwhile, do you know if your mother is going to do anything about getting the rights back from The King's Men to all his plays?

Yours sincerely,

Luke Strong

Artistic Director Emeritus

February 3rd '23

Dear Mrs Shakespeare,

FOLIO

I presume it is you, Anne – may I call you Anne? Or
Agnes?– who, as the widow, are behind the commissioning
of the forthcoming, delayed Folio publication? You're to be
congratulated on reviving interest in 18 plays which weren't
otherwise published in your husband's lifetime: *The Taming
of the Shrew*, *The Two Gentlemen of Verona*, *Henry VI Part 1*,
The Comedy of Errors, *King John*, *As You Like It*, *Julius Caesar*,
Twelfth Night, *Measure for Measure*, *All's Well That Ends Well*,
Timon of Athens, *Macbeth*, *Antony & Cleopatra*, *Coriolanus*,
Cymbeline, *The Winter's Tale*, *The Tempest* and *All Is True: Henry
VIII*.

William's buried in your local church, with that verse hokum as
his epitaph:

> "GOOD FRIEND FOR IESVS SAKE FORBEARE
> TO DIGG THE DVST ENCLOASED HEARE.
> BLESE BE YE MAN YT SPARES THES STONES,
> AND CVRST BE HE YT MOVES MY BONES."

Were you hurt that he wasn't buried in Westminster Abbey, while
Francis Beaumont, who passed away a month earlier, was?
Beaumont is the first playwright to be honoured with eternal
accommodation in Poet's Corner. William was a "star of poets",
as Ben Jonson says in his dedicatory poem to the Folio; but
clearly the "constellation" is crowded! Jonson goes on to say
that it's too common to be one of the dead gang in Westminster
Abbey:

> "   I will *not* lodge thee by
> Chaucer or Spenser, or bid Beaumont lie
> A little further to make thee a room.
> Thou art a monument without a tomb."

Your husband wrote for the ear and not the eye. Hugh Holland's dedicatory poem in the Folio preface is addressed:

> "Upon the lines and life of the famous scenic poet Master William Shakespeare."

In our world now it's hard for us to appreciate his scenic poetry to the full, hard to recapture the kind of imagination with which he was engaging. I don't mean your world of a market town in the provincial West Midlands: sadly that's all too familiar to too many of us in our small-minded, Little England, complacent, non-metropolitan lives. I'm talking about the vivid world of London, a nexus of creeds and cultures and commerce that your husband used as his mixing palette, his melting pot. He had the vision to paint such extraordinary pictures in his audience's mind's eye that I doubt we now have the wherewithal to see them and appreciate them in all their glory. In our all-seeing, all-knowing world, our mind's eyes are in danger of becoming blurry, if not blind.

Your husband writes the *mise-en-scène* into the words, words which were largely performed in daylight, in open-roofed theatres, until the winter seasons at the indoor theatre at Blackfriars from the end of the 'Noughties. Time and again in our modern theatre a company comes along and rediscovers this about his plays: that they suffer when over-burdened with production values as we try to keep up with the Inigo Joneses. Your husband thrusts the actor and the spoken word centre stage. It's a massively simple idea. It requires actors and audiences to be exposed to a scale of performance to match the size of that idea. This can be effective in the intensity of a small Studio theatre; although this is timid in comparison with the bolder uncluttered space of the thrust stage or lyric playhouse.

Your husband's writing is motored by the power of the spoken word. In the depths of nihilistic despair in *King Lear*, Edgar articulates a kind of hope:

> "   The worst is not
>   So long as we can say 'This is the worst'." (IVi)

I hope you'll do well out of the sales of the Folio. After all, having left you to raise the children alone in Stratford while he hacked out a living as a writer and indulged his bug for acting 100 miles away in London, William certainly owes you one.

Yours sincerely,

Luke Strong

Artistic Director Emeritus

◇◇◇

November 11th '23

Dear Mr Heminge and Mr Condell,

FOLIO

I am sorry that Anne Shakespeare has passed away before the final publication of her late husband's Folio of works. It was a shame that the Jaggards halted the printing they started last year because they had a rush job on for an order of greater importance to them: William Burton's *Description of Leicester*. And then very sad that William Jaggard died a month ago, on the eve of publication, his son Isaac taking the credit on the title page alongside Ed Blount. William Jaggard had been your regular publisher, printing all The King's Men's playbills.

But here it is at long last and it certainly is a mighty achievement. However, I do have a few bones to pick with you!

1) You claim to have put together this folio edition of Shakespeare's poems and plays

> "without ambition either for self-profit or fame; only to keep the memory of so worthy a friend and fellow alive as was our Shakespeare".

If you are not to profit from the enterprise, why do you entreat "The Great Variety of Readers" to get their money out – not once, not twice, but three times?:

> "The fate of all books depends on your capacities; and not of your heads alone, but of your purses [1] … You will stand for your privileges, we know, – to read and censure. Do so, but buy it first [2]. That doth best commend a book, the stationer says… But whatever you do, buy [3]."

"Buy … Buy": it's a fairly blunt sales pitch, you'll admit. At the same time, you attempt to corner the market by killing off the competition:

> "Before you were abused with divers stolen and surreptitious copies, maim'd and deform'd by the frauds and stealths of injurious imposters."

2) I'm sure you mean well, but you're both in danger of doing a disservice to Shakespeare, and to all writers, by immortalising him as a poet-playwright who wouldn't deign to get his hands dirty:

> "He was a happy imitator of Nature, was a most gentle expresser of it: his mind and hand went together; and what he thought, he utter'd with that easiness, that we have scarce received from him a blot in his papers."

Come off it! The manuscripts were 'fouled' by blottings and scribblings and amendments. The only piece of dramatic writing of Shakespeare's which survives in his hand is his contribution to *Sir Thomas More*: it's smudged and splattered all over. There is something nose-wrinkling about the term 'foul papers', isn't there, as if it's an unfortunate aberration on an otherwise perfect genius, the deliberate flaw in the magic carpet, the natural imperfection in the diamond? I like to think of these papers not as 'foul' but as fairly messy – working documents, scrawled and scribbled and doodled all over when inspiration failed to come, and written with a stream-of-consciousness haste, spelling mistakes and all, when the ideas flowed. Jonson's dedicatory poem gets nearer to it by likening William to an artisan-artist, a spinner of yarns, a weaver of tales:

"Nature herself was proud of his designs,
And joy'd to wear the dressing of his lines
Which were so richly spun and woven so fit."

Jonson the craftsman recognises his colleague's effort:

"For a good poet's made as well as born
… Shakespeare's mind and manners brightly shines
In his well-turned and true-filed lines."

3) Jonson makes another good point that publishing the Folio keeps Shakespeare's spirit alive:

"   While thy book doth live
And we have wits to read and praise to give…
He was not of an age but for all time."

In praising Shakespeare, he also takes a sideswipe at the dead competition:

"   Thou didst our Lyly outshine,
Or sporting Kyd, or Marlowe's mighty line."

But you two are more aggressive, telling us if we don't like what we read in your book, then we just don't get it:

"Read him, therefore; and again and again: and if then you do not like him, surely you are in some manifest danger not to understand him".

4) Where the *de facto* inaugural Poet Laureate, Ben Jonson, published his collection of plays in 1616 under the characteristically utilitarian title *Works*, you have gone and categorised Shakespeare's plays with more of a grandiose flourish: 'Tragedies, Histories and Comedies'. It's a real pain because it will be the starting point for so much generalised discussion of Shakespeare's plays! Are they tragic with a bit of comedy? Or historical with a bit of tragedy? And as for the

pastoral... I'm sure the irony of such reductive pigeon-holing is not lost on you – see Polonius':

> "Tragedy, comedy, history, pastoral, pastoral-comical, historical-pastoral, tragical-historical, tragical-comical-historical-pastoral ..." (*Hamlet*, IIii)

5) Why Folio? There's a proliferation of Quartos from all the Elizabethan and Jacobean playwrights. They're printed on smaller, cheaper pieces of paper than the overpriced 'rag' paper, hand-made in and imported from Normandy that make up the Folio size. The Folio is also a thick tome. Quartos are readily usable as scripts in rehearsal rather than just as prestigious reference-books for the well-appointed home or library. I know Quartos are usually flawed editions, rushed into print and often without permission, those so-called "Bad" Quartos, unapproved by Shakespeare or The Chamberlain's/King's Men. (You recently had your work cut out curtailing Thomas Pavier's unauthorised Shakespeare Quartos Collection of 1619.) As just the playwright, Shakespeare wouldn't have collected a royalty for a Quarto. But they are instant play-scripts reflecting theatre practice, in my experience of working with them – more so, perhaps, than this Folio. Quartos appear not long after the plays are premièred, meeting a public demand for a copy of the play they've just heard. They are living documents, so although they may be peppered with inaccuracies, they reflect the shifting, impermanent nature of theatre. And I bet Shakespeare proudly collected and cherished each one, maybe even bought them for his Mum (if she could read) and Dad, and for the kids.

6) Whose are the stage directions in the Folio? In *Titus Andronicus* the stage directions seem too detailed for an apprentice, Elizabethan playwright. Do they reflect Jacobean theatre practice more than the original writer's intentions? Or are they rudimentary guides to reading by editors? Throughout the Folio, the word 'Flourish' is used a lot – meaning, presumably, a bright fanfare to herald someone's arrival, such is the taste in Jacobean theatre; theatre companies employ loads of

trumpeters nowadays. But when rehearsing Shakespeare's plays, the implicit staging is frequently revealed within the dialogue and in the spatial relationships played out on stage. Stage directions in Shakespeare's plays are, in practice, redundant.

Thanks.

Yours,

Luke Strong

Artistic Director Emeritus

◇◇◇

March 27th '25

To the Editor

Dear Sir,

As we enter a new era of Caroline meritocracy under the new King, I would like to suggest having a handy five-star system for all of William Shakespeare's plays so that we know which ones are a must-see, a no-brainer, a so-so, a stinker, etc.

Thus:

The Taming of the Shrew	*
Henry VI Part 1	**
Henry VI Part 2	***
Henry VI Part 3	****
The Two Gentlemen of Verona	***
Titus Andronicus	*****
Richard III	****
The Comedy of Errors	****
Love's Labour's Lost	*
A Midsummer Night's Dream	*****
Romeo & Juliet	*****
King John	**
Richard II	****

The Merchant of Venice	–	(can you have negative stars?)
Henry IV Part 1	***	
Henry IV Part 2	*****	
The Merry Wives of Windsor	*****	(only kidding: it's crap)
Much Ado About Nothing	****	
As You Like It	***	
Henry V	***	
Julius Caesar	***	
Hamlet	*****	
Sir Thomas More	*	
Twelfth Night	****	
Troilus & Cressida	*	
Othello	***	
Measure for Measure	***	
All's Well That Ends Well	*	
Timon of Athens	*	
King Lear	*****	
Macbeth	*****	
Antony & Cleopatra	**	
Coriolanus	**	
Pericles	*	
Cymbeline	***	
The Winter's Tale	****	
The Tempest	****	
All is True: Henry VIII	*	
The Two Noble Kinsmen	**	

Yours faithfully,

Horatio J. Dowden-Adams

Dramaturg (retired)

1558	Elizabeth becomes queen	
1564	February: Marlowe born	
	April: Shakespeare born	
	Plague in Stratford kills 200	
1570	Father found guilty of usury	
1582	Marries Anne Hathaway	
1583	Daughter Susannah born	
1585	Twins Judith & Hamnet born	
	Amleth	Anonymous
1588	Spanish Armada	
	Arden of Faversham	Anonymous
1589	*Famous Victories of Henry V*	Anonymous
	Taming of the Shrew [F]	
	Taming of a Shrew	Anon Q 1592
1590	*Mucedorus*	Anonymous
1591	*Henry VI 2*	co-authorship
	Henry VI 3	co-authorship
	Two Gents of Verona [F]	
	Titus Andronicus	+ George Peele
1592	*Henry VI 1* [F]	+ Nashe/Greene/Peele
	Edward III	co-authorship
	Fair Em, Miller's Daughter	Robert Wilson
	June: Plague closes theatres	
	Richard III	
1593	*Edmund Ironside*	Anonymous
	Venus & Adonis	
	Marlowe dies	
	Rape of Lucrece	
	Sonnets begun	
1594	Summer: Theatres Re-open	
	Comedy of Errors [F]	

1595	*Love's Labour's Lost*	
	Love's Labour's Won	Lost
	Locrine	Anonymous
	A Midsummer Night's Dream	
	Romeo & Juliet	
	King John [F]	
1596	August: Hamnet drowns	
	Richard II	
	Merchant of Venice	
	Henry IV 1	
1597	*Isle of Dogs*	Jonson/Nashe + others
	Theatres closed	
	Merry Wives of Windsor	
	Henry IV 2	
1598	*Much Ado About Nothing*	
1599	*Henry V*	
	As You Like It [F]	
	Julius Caesar [F]	
	The Passionate Pilgrim	2 Shakespeare sonnets
1600	*England's Parnassus*	100 Shakespeare quotations
1601	Essex Rebellion	
	Sir Thomas More	+ Munday, Chettle, Dekker, Heywood
	The Phoenix & the Turtle	
	September: Father dies	
	Hamlet	
	Twelfth Night [F]	
	Troilus & Cressida	
1602	*Merry Devil of Edmonton*	Dekker, Ford & Rowley
1603	Elizabeth dies	
	James crowned	
1603-04	May to April: Plague	

1604	*Othello*	
	Measure [F]	+ Middleton additions
	The London Prodigal	Anonymous
	Puritan, Widow of Watling St	Anonymous
1605	*All's Well* [F]	
	Timon [F]	+ Middleton
	King Lear	2 versions
1606-10	Plague (except April-July 08)	
1606	*Macbeth* [F]	+ Middleton additions
	Antony & Cleopatra [F]	
	A Yorkshire Tragedy	Anonymous
1608	*Coriolanus* [F]	
	February: Granddaughter Elizabeth born	
	The Birth of Merlin	William Rowley +
	September: Mother dies	
	Pericles	+ George Wilkins
1609	*Sonnets* published + *A Lover's Complaint*	
1610	*Cymbeline* [F]	
1611	*Winter's Tale* [F]	
	Tempest [F]	
1612	*Cardenio*	+ Fletcher (lost)
1613	*Henry VIII* [F]	+ Fletcher
	Two Noble Kinsmen	+ Fletcher
1616	Shakespeare dies April 23rd	
1619	Collected Q edition foiled	
1623	Spring: Anne dies	
	Autumn: Folio published	
1625	James dies; Charles crowned	

F = first published in the First Folio, 1623
Q = Quarto publication

SELECT BIBLIOGRAPHY

Shakespeare Complete Works:

The RSC/Macmillan 2007, eds. Jonathan Bate & Eric Rasmussen (especially influential)

The Oxford 1986, eds. Stanley Wells & Gary Taylor (the benchmark)

The Wordsworth 1996, based on Shakespeare Head Press, Oxford Edition (portable)

Shakespeare Plays:

Anthonie, and Cleopatra, Prentice Hall 1995, ed. John Turner

Coriolanus, Arden2 1976, ed. Philip Brockbank

Cymbeline, Arden2 1955, ed. J. M. Nosworthy

Edward III, New Cambridge 1998, ed. Giorgio Melchiori

Hamlet, New Cambridge 1985, ed. Philip Edwards

The Three-Text Hamlet, New York 1991, eds. Paul Bertram & Bernice W. Kliman

Henry VI Part 1, Arden3 2000, ed. Edward Burns

Henry VIII, Arden2 1957, ed. R. A. Foakes

Henry VIII, Arden3 2000, ed. Gordon McMullan

King Lear, Arden2 1977, ed. Kenneth Muir

Merchant of Venice, Arden2 1959, ed. John Russell Brown

Merry Wives of Windsor, New Cambridge 2000, ed. Giorgio Melchiori

A Midsummer Night's Dream, Oxford 1994, ed. Peter Holland

Much Ado About Nothing, Arden2 1981, ed. A. R. Humphreys

Richard II, New Cambridge 1985, ed. Andrew Gurr

Sir Thomas More, Manchester 1990, eds. Vittorio Gabrielli & Giorgio Melchiori

The Tempest, Arden3 1999, ed. Virginia Mason Vaughan & Alden T. Vaughan

The Tempest, Arden2 1954, ed. Frank Kermode

Timon of Athens, New Penguin 1970, ed. G. R. Hibbard

Titus Andronicus, Arden3 1995, ed. Jonathan Bate

Two Noble Kinsmen, New Penguin 1977, ed. N. W. Bawcutt

The Winter's Tale, Arden2 1963, ed. J. H. P. Pafford

Shakespeare Screenplays:

Henry V, Chatto & Windus 1989, adapt. Kenneth Branagh

Other Plays:

Arden of Faversham, 'Anonymous', New Mermaids 1982, ed. Martin White

Ted Hughes's Tales from Ovid, adapted by Tim Supple & Simon Reade, Faber 1999

Christopher Marlowe: The Complete Plays, Penguin 1969, ed. J.B. Steane

The Herbal Bed, Peter Whelan, Warner/Chappell 1996

Other Poetry:

Chaucer: Complete Works, Oxford 1974, ed. F.N. Robinson

Ovid's Metamorphoses, Arthur Golding 1567/ www.elizabethanauthors.com 2002

Other Screenplays:

Shakespeare in Love, Marc Norman and Tom Stoppard, Faber 1998

Shakespeare Reference:

The Genius of Shakespeare, Jonathan Bate, Picador 1997

Soul of the Age, Jonathan Bate, Viking Penguin 2008

The First Folio of Shakespeare, Peter W. M. Bayney, Folger Library publications 1991

Shakespeare: The Invention of the Human, Howard Bloom, Fourth Estate 1999

The TLS on Shakespeare, eds. Michael Caines & Mick Imlah, TLS 2003

The Complete Concordance to Shakespeare, Mrs Cowden-Clarke, Bickers & Son 1881

Political Shakespeare, eds. Jonathan Dollimore & Alan Sinfield, Manchester 1985

Will & Me, Dominic Dromgoole, Allen Lane 2006

Henslowe's Diaries, ed. R.A. Foakes & R.T. Rickert, Cambridge University Press 1961

A Short Guide to Shakespeare's Plays, John Goodwin,
Heineman 1979

Will in the World, Stephen Greenblatt, Pimlico 2005

Shakespeare's Wife, Germaine Greer, Bloomsbury 2007

A Pocket Guide to Shakespeare's Plays, Kenneth McLeish &
Stephen Unwin, Faber 1998

The Shakespeare Myth, ed. Graham Holderness, Manchester 1988

The Lodger: Shakespeare on Silver Street, Charles Nicholl,
Allen Lane 2007

Shakespeare The Thinker, A.D. Nuttall, Yale University Press 2007

1599: A Year in the Life of William Shakespeare, James Shapiro,
Faber 2005

Shakespeare's Professional Career, Peter Thomson,
Cambridge University Press 1992

Other Reference:

12 Books That Changed The World, Melvyn Bragg,
Hodder & Stoughton 2006

Cheek by Jowl: Ten Years of Celebration, Simon Reade,
Absolute Classics 1991

Letters to George, Max Stafford-Clark, Nick Hern Books 1989

A South Indian Journey, Michael Wood, Penguin 2007

ACKNOWLEDGEMENTS

Some of this material was first aired in public lectures and panel discussions delivered in Valencia, Helsinki, Ann Arbor, Detroit, Edinburgh, Newcastle-upon-Tyne, Stratford-upon-Avon, Exeter, and London; in published reviews and articles contributed to *Venue Magazine*, *City Limits*, *Time Out*, *Plays International*, *Guardian*, *Financial Times*; and in notes compiled for directors and for audiences at the Royal Shakespeare Company and at Bristol Old Vic.

For their influential thoughts on Shakespeare over the years and other ideas in this book, thanks to: Allison Abbate, Biyi Bandele, Jonathan Bate, Cicely Berry, Michael Billington, Michael Bogdanov, Laurence Boswell, Robert Bowman, Clive Brill, Jonathan Broadbent, Tom Cairns, David Calder, John Cannon, Michael Coveney, Simon Curtis, Stephen Daldry, Andrew Davies, Philippa Davies, David Fielding, Sean Foley, Sunila Galappatti, Paul Godfrey, Christopher Good, Sasha Hails, Lee Hall, Michael Hastings, Marc von Henning, Craig Higginson, Jeremy Howe, Terry Johnson, Lesley Ann Jones, Toby Jones, Nicholas de Jongh, Jonathan Kent, Miles Ketley, Jeremy Kingston, David Lan, Chris Larner, Patrick Li, Maggie Lunn, Caroline Maude, Alastair Macaulay, Anthony Macilwaine, Danny Moar, Patrick Moriarty, Jessica Munns, Peter New, Pat O'Connor, Steve Philips, Tom Piper, Stephen Poliakoff, Lindsay Posner, Esther Richardson, Ginny Schiller, Amelia Sears, Austin Shaw, Timothy Sheader, Antony Sher, David Snodin, Melly Still, Paul Taylor, Anne Tipton, Ulrich Tukur, David Tushingham, Matthew Warcus, Julian Webber, Samuel West, Bill Wilkinson, Steven Wilkins, Ralph G. Williams, Denise Wood, Nicholas Wright; Mary & Graham Anderson; Peter Corbin & Douglas Sedge; Declan Donnellan & Nick Ormerod; Peter Thomson and Chris McCullough; Barbara A. Mowat, Folger Shakespeare Library; Peter Holland, Stanley Wells and Russell Jackson, Shakespeare Institute and Shakespeare Centre, Stratford-upon-Avon; Michael Attenborough, Michael Boyd, Gregory Doran and Adrian Noble. And to the late Alan Bates, Michael Fitch, Nathan Joseph, Kenneth McLeish, Adrian Mitchell, Steven Pimlott, Paul Reade and Gareth Roberts:

"O Gentlemen! The time of life is short" (*Henry IV Part 1*).

For encouragement and specific help with this book, thanks to: Dominic Dromgoole, David Farr, Mark Leipacher, Ferdy Roberts, Tim Supple; Ann & Dan Reid; Hugh & Pippa Stables; Jane Tassell, Royal

Shakespeare Company; St John Donald & Georgina Lewis, United Agents; Theatre Royal, Bath; Batemans Trust, India; and to Clare & Michael Morpurgo for constant inspiration.

Special thanks to: James Hogan, Daisy Bowie-Sell, James Stephens, Stephen Watson and all at Oberon for their guidance; Alison Reid for her perception and insight; Amy, Otto and Rose Reade for their challenging thoughts; Hazel Reade for her Lily Strong letter; and to Ken Ludwig, for his timely and emboldening enthusiasm.

Apologies to anyone pilfered, paraphrased or parodied.

Simon Reade
Chennai – Le Theil – Bristol
2008/2009

BIOGRAPHY OF SIMON READE

Simon Reade read English at Exeter University where he was President of Student Theatre. He was Literary Manager of the Gate Theatre, London 1990-1993 and Literary Manager & Dramaturg at the Royal Shakespeare Company 1997-2001. RSC dramaturgy includes the Shakespeare History Play cycle *This England: The Histories, Hamlet* (starring Samuel West), *Richard III* (starring Robert Lindsay), Ben Jonson's *Bartholomew Fair* and *Volpone*, Schiller's *Don Carlos* and Aphra Behn's *Oroonoko*. He also co-abridged Shaw's *Back to Methuselah* with David Fielding (publ. Oberon). At the RSC he commissioned, developed and produced new plays by April de Angelis, Biyi Bandele, Moira Buffini, David Farr, David Greig, Lee Hall, Zinnie Harris, Martin McDonagh, Adrian Mitchell and Stephen Poliakoff amongst others.

As Artistic Director of Bristol Old Vic 2003-2007, Simon produced five award-winning seasons including five Shakespeares, new plays and classic adaptations by Ranjit Bolt, Nick Dear, Carol Ann Duffy, David Farr, Toby Farrow, Sasha Hails, Lee Hall, Toby Hulse, Ken Ludwig, Frank McGuinness and Annie Siddons, popular revivals of *The Rivals*, *Les Liaisons Dangereuses*, Rodgers and Hammerstein's *Cinderella* and Stoppard's *Arcadia*, and controversial productions of Marlowe's *Tamburlaine* and *Doctor Faustus* and an all-male *Importance of Being Earnest*. He directed *Cyrano de Bergerac*, acclaimed productions of Pinter's *The Birthday Party*, *The Dumb Waiter* and *The Room* (50th Anniversary Production) and his own multi-award-winning adaptations of Michael Morpurgo's *Private Peaceful* and Geraldine McCaughrean's *Not the End of the World* (both publ. Oberon). He was also the founding producer of Mayfest, Bristol's annual celebration of physical and visual theatre, and co-produced with the likes of Kneehigh, Headlong, West Yorkshire Playhouse, Lyric Hammersmith, Birmingham Rep., Liverpool Theatres, Young Vic, B.I.T.E. and Travelling Light.

He directs the Michael Morpugo concert series and most recently he adapted and directed Philip Pullman's *The Scarecrow and His Servant* (publ. Oberon) at Southwark Playhouse. His other adaptations include Michael Morpurgo's *The Mozart Question, Alice's Adventures in Wonderland* (TMA Award: Best Show for Young People), Philip Pullman's *Aladdin and The Enchanted Lamp* (with Aletta Collins – publ. Oberon) and, with Tim Supple, Ted Hughes' *Tales from Ovid* and Salman Rushdie's *Midnight's*

Children, both for the RSC. At the RSC he also directed and co-wrote *Epitaph for the Official Secrets Act* with Paul Greengrass. His plays have been seen in New York, Ann Arbor, Dublin, Stockholm, Chennai, London, Bristol and Edinburgh and toured in Sweden, the USA and across the UK.

Simon has also worked in television at the BBC and for Tiger Aspect Productions, and extensively as a cultural commentator in broadcast and print media. His previous books include a history of the international touring company Cheek by Jowl (publ. Absolute Classics). He is the Director of Poonamallee Productions and is currently Associate Producer for Theatre Royal Bath Productions.